Everything that follows is based on recent, real-life experience that has been proven to work

Professional Survival Solutions

James Shepherd-Barron

THREE RIVERS PRESS
NEW YORK

Copyright © 2010 by James Shepherd-Barron

All rights reserved.
Published in the United States by Three Rivers Press, an imprint of the Crown Publishing Group, a division of Random House, Inc., New York.
www.crownpublishing.com

Three Rivers Press and the Tugboat design are registered trademarks of Random House, Inc.

Originally published in Great Britain by Particular Books, an imprint of Penguin Press, a division of Penguin Books Ltd, London, in 2010.

Library of Congress Cataloging-in-Publication Data

Shepherd-Barron, James.
Everything that follows is based on recent, real-life experience that has been proven to work: professional survival solutions / James Shepherd-Barron—1st ed.
p. cm.
1. Survival skills. 2. Humanitarian assistance. 3. International relief. I. Title.
GF86.S536 2011
613.6'9—dc22   2010047592

ISBN 978-0-307-88632-3
eISBN 978-0-307-88633-0

Printed in the United States of America

Book design by Richard Marston

10 9 8 7 6 5 4 3 2 1

First U.S. Edition

This book is dedicated to all those humanitarians who have sacrificed themselves while selflessly seeking to make the world a better place. People like Chris Klein-Beekman and Sergio Vieira de Mello, who were tragically murdered in the August 2003 bombing of the United Nations office in Baghdad less than twenty-four hours after I had been with them.

They, and others like them, remain my inspiration.

The book is also dedicated to my two children, Rory and Sam, who may one day understand what their dad has been up to all these years and forgive the long absences. And who might, at the same time, find the contents of this book of some use.

Acknowledgments

The author wishes to thank the humanitarian experts who contributed to the writing of this handbook, especially Joseph Ashmore and Julia Macro, who helped develop the original idea, and John Adlam, Stacey Winston, Kate Crawford, Brian Kelly, Andrew Macleod, Anna Pont, Wolfgang Gressman, Nicolaas de Zwagger, Mark Cutts, Bibi Lamond, Dave Hodgkin, Tom Corsellis, Jack Jones, Aoibheann O'Keeffe, Emma Jowett, Craig Hampton, Laetitia Weibel, Andrew Roberts, Marcus Browell, Ben Verbeke and Jyri Rantanen, who provided invaluable technical advice based on their own field experience.

The author would also like to thank the following, who volunteered their time in order to make this project a reality: Tom Colborne Malpas, Antoinette Sharp, Piers and Sophie Lawson, Nick and Susie Fenwick Clennel, Michael Robinson, Quentin and Isabell Browell, Robert Scott Moncrieff and Jane Hampson.

And finally, none of this would have made it into print if I hadn't stumbled across the best literary agent a first-time author could ever hope for, Caroline Michel of PfD, and if I hadn't been introduced to the calm authority of Helen Conford and her capable team at Penguin, including Rebecca, Mari, Jessie and Nikki. Thanks to you all for your patience in showing me the way.

Contents

5. Getting There

How to deal with…

6. Driving

How to deal with…

7. Managing

How to deal with…

Appendix: Checklists

Introduction

This handbook was conceived in the snow-clad Karakoram mountains, where I was helping coordinate relief operations following the devastating earthquake of 2005 in Kashmir. Tens of thousands lay trapped, either dead or dying, under the rubble of their schools, offices and homes, with millions more wandering homeless.

I had worked in similar disaster zones around the world, and it became painfully obvious to me that once more too many of the wonderful people arriving to work for the hundreds of aid agencies that had flocked to the area to provide assistance did not know how to cope with the grim realities facing them and were, themselves, in need of support. Less than five years later I watched history repeat itself in Haiti.

Aid work is extremely demanding, both physically and mentally. It demands more than testosterone and adrenaline to help you through the harsh living conditions, exhaustion and emotional highs and lows of working with the victims of disaster; it demands a range of skills and coping mechanisms that can be taught. Yet many of the professional aid workers—let alone the volunteers—I was working alongside in Kashmir had received minimal, if any, training in the basic techniques of survival. Despite this, they had been pitched at a few hours' notice into working eighteen-hour days and seven-day weeks surrounded by sights, sounds and smells of immense suffering in sub-zero conditions where food, water and shelter were in short supply.

I had seen the same thing in Darfur the year before, and in Bosnia, Rwanda, Kosovo and Iraq before that, where similar threats to an individual's safety and sanity were frequently compounded by aggressive men waving guns around.

Having resolved to do something to help redress this apparent shortcoming within the aid community, I didn't start writing until a forced stay in the hospital two years later allowed me the time. During the months of rehabilitation that followed, the manuscript grew as I committed my experiences and lessons learned to paper. With friends and colleagues commenting on early drafts, it quickly became apparent that the book was resonating with them in some unforeseen way and that the anecdotes and advice it contained appeared to be of practical value to a much wider and less adrenaline-dependent audience, an audience wanting simply to experience remoter parts of the world without being exposed to unnecessary risk.

I was reminded, too, that the aid community comprises international and national staff employed by UN agencies, nongovernmental organizations, the Red Cross movement and others for their wide range of technical qualifications—as communicators, analysts, coordinators, doctors, public-health planners, water-sanitation engineers and architects, for example—and not for their survival skills. And that all of these highly qualified people are supported by auxiliary staff such as drivers, translators, guards, IT technicians, radio operators, vehicle mechanics, back-office administrators and so on, many of whom are also required to work from time to time in "deep-field" conditions.

Surrounding the aid community are myriad other professions, too, principal among whom are the media with all their foreign correspondents and production teams, the diplomatic corps, international donors and, not far behind, the commercial sector with their "corporate social responsibility" budgets and sales executives looking for reconstruction opportunities.

And as the father of two then-teenagers, it also dawned on me that a whole generation of socially aware and motivated young people were not just traveling through ever-more remote regions before or after going to college but were seeking something more meaningful to do along the way by which their life skills would be developed and their future chances of employment enhanced. Spending a few months or more as a volunteer with an aid agency in the field seemed to be their work experience of choice. But school leavers have little experience of how to survive or what coping strategies to employ when the going gets tough.

At the same time, my friends, their parents, seemed to be becoming more and more concerned by the apparently increasing risks involved in undertaking such adventures.

"Unless," they said, "our children deliberately choose to join the military, become war correspondents or do humanitarian work, we don't expect them to be blown up or shot at." Yet the risks of these and other such things happening to us or our children when abroad *appears* to be increasing: traveling students are robbed and raped in Tanzania, tourists bombed in India, cricketers shot at in Pakistan, oil workers held hostage in Nigeria and business executives abducted in Colombia.

They agreed that working as a volunteer in a Romanian orphanage when an H1N1 swine flu outbreak is declared, conducting research in a quiet Beirut suburb when Israeli air-strikes roar in overhead, having dinner in a South Asian hotel when a suicide truck bomber tries to drive through the gates or lying on a beach in the Pacific when a tsunami approaches no longer seem like far-fetched scenarios.

So, are they right? Have the risks increased? Is backpacking around the world more dangerous now than it was ten years ago? Does volunteering for an aid agency mean increased likelihood of being blown to smithereens by a suicide bomber? Is being a foreign correspondent to invite execution by some gun-toting zealot on prime-time television? Are diplomats and business executives destined to spend years tied up in the jungle as hostages?

Vastly increased media coverage ensures that we all hear all the horror stories all the time. This fuels the impression that the world is indeed much less safe than it was a few years ago. But while the actual number of incidents has certainly increased over the past decade, so has the number of people venturing into these potentially hostile situations. This means that the *relative* risk of being caught up in someone else's violent event has increased only marginally. It may well be, however, that this is no longer the case in parts of Afghanistan, Pakistan and Somalia, as recent years have seen a clear escalation in the number of incidents involving, if not deliberately targeting, foreigners in these particular places.

To compound the man-made risks of travel, the frequency and ferocity of natural disaster is on the rise. According to the Red Cross, the number of disasters has grown by 60 percent since the early nineties, with 657 natural and technological disasters reported in 2008 affecting 281 million people worldwide. Of these, eighteen events—nine floods, four windstorms, four droughts and one wildfire—

affected more than one million people each. With the exception of three droughts in Africa, all of these disasters occurred in Asia.

Meanwhile, Reporters Without Borders reports that a total of 60 journalists were murdered and 29 kidnapped over the same period— mostly in Iraq and Afghanistan—with more than 1,500 media workers arrested, threatened or physically attacked in connection with their work elsewhere in the world.

This book cannot explain what aid work entails. Nor can it hope to cover the sort of survival skills needed when lost in the wilderness with nothing but a sharp stick for company. But what it can and does do is outline the sorts of hazards and risks facing those contemplating working or traveling abroad—in whatever capacity—and suggest ways of mitigating those risks.

Recognizing and then mitigating risk is your affair.

As an aid professional myself, perhaps my personal experience would be useful in illustrating the sort of risks and hazards we all might one day be facing. In Darfur, I gave a live radio interview, crossed a front-line minefield, recovered a bogged vehicle, administered first aid to a deep wound, trained health workers to give polio vaccinations, negotiated with a rebel warlord and set up a helicopter night-landing site—all in the same day.

In Baghdad, I have had to jump in the bath to take cover from ricocheting bullets. I have built an airstrip in Burundi, helped deliver a baby to a Rwandan refugee on a Congolese roadside and navigated to safety when lost in the deserts of Chad.

Testosterone-fueled machismo mixed with a heady cocktail of cordite, adrenaline and radio static—all stirred with a whiff of moral superiority—is not the impression I am trying to convey with such tales. Nor is the use of the personal pronoun meant to imply anything special. The message is simply that each activity described above, and outlined in more detail in this book, demands a degree of basic knowledge over and above the technical skills that see aid professionals mobilized in the first place.

And while it may, admittedly, be a little different to do all these things on one day, and some of the situations are relatively extreme, there is nothing inherently unusual about any of them: aid workers, diplomats, drivers, translators, journalists and those working alongside them get into these situations and confront these sorts of challenges on a regular basis—especially if they are working in conflict zones.

When abroad, it is as well to be aware of the worst that could happen and to prepare accordingly. With that in mind, you might at least want to consider how to mitigate the risks of an unpleasant outcome should you walk into that worst-case scenario. This book is for you.

The procedures described in this book are general guidelines only for use in emergency situations where no support is available. Always seek professional help wherever possible, use your common sense and take precautions to avoid hazardous situations.

It has been compiled with the advice of friends and colleagues who have had cause to do the things described, either to save their own lives or the lives (and sanity) of others while working and traveling in some of the most challenging and hazardous places on the planet. Everything that follows is based on recent, real-life experience and has been proven to work. It does not set out, therefore, to be politically correct, just effective.

In hoping you find it useful one day, I wish you a safe trip.

Chapter 1

Deep Field

How to deal with...

The United Nations refers to "deep field" as being in those places where relief and development operations take place beyond the outskirts of major towns. In Darfur, deep-field operations are ongoing in refugee camps far from ramshackle mud-walled towns such as El Geneina. During earthquake-relief operations in Pakistan, humanitarian teams lived and worked through the winter with disaster-affected populations at high altitude where resupply was only possible by helicopter—the mountain tracks were too steep even for mules. In large swaths of sub-Saharan Africa, it takes hours in a small plane to get to a doctor. These are typical deep-field situations.

... **angry animals**

REALITY CHECK

In Burundi early in 1995, the daughter of a Russian diplomat was swimming with her family on the north shore of Lake Tanganyika when she was grabbed by an enormous crocodile. This fearsome creature has the most powerful bite of all animals, exerting two tons of pressure. According to witnesses—who were in shock even weeks later—the girl was eaten alive while the family tried to pull her from its jaws. What a way to go. It will be no consolation to the family that there *are* ways to get a crocodile to open its mouth in such circumstances—though it has to be said, it would be a brave person who tried it.

If someone is grabbed by a hungry crocodile, **hit it hard on the end of its snout and/or punch its eyes**. For this to work, you will have to immobilize the monster first. According to crocodile hunters in Australia, all you have to do to achieve this is sit on its back, cover its eyes and pull its legs off the ground!

REALITY CHECK

Hippos used to wander the main streets of Bujumbura, Burundi, in the late evening, in search of fresh grazing. As we were under curfew and had to be back in our compounds by nightfall, I rarely saw this. But running late one evening—something one should never do when trigger-happy soldiers are manning checkpoints in the middle of a war zone—we came across a hippo lumbering down the street with its baby. Without hesitation, it charged our car, nearly turning us over and making a large dent in the side. Happily, we could drive on out of its way, so it lost interest. There was some trouble explaining the damage to a skeptical operations manager the next morning, however.

The biggest killer of humans in Africa is not the crocodile, however. Neither is it the lion. It is the **hippopotamus**. (Mosquitoes are responsible for killing many more people, but, as the vector of the *Plasmodium* parasite, only indirectly.) Hippos have poor eyesight but large teeth. If you are charged, you have probably inadvertently put yourself between the hippo and its baby or the water. **If out in the open, stand your ground and dodge to one side at the last possible moment.** Keep doing this until it gets bored. As long as there is only one such animal intent on goring, trampling or tearing you to death, you can do this as many times as it takes until the animal tires and wanders off. And it will. **If there is cover, get behind it. If you can, climb a tree** but keep in mind that large animals with claws—and this includes bears—are good tree climbers.

Big cats have better eyesight than we do, run faster than we do and are generally more agile than we are, especially on the run. They also have claws, so neither running away nor dodging will work—not unless you run as a group and sacrifice someone who runs slower than you. Nor will climbing a tree. When faced with a snarling, spitting, about-to-pounce big cat (lion, tiger, puma, leopard, etc.), the only thing to do is **stand still, making as much noise as you can while making yourself appear as large as you can. Open your clothing and flap it wildly. If that doesn't frighten the cat off, try throwing it whatever food you have within reach while backing off slowly.** Turning your back on an advancing big cat, or even crouching down, is to invite it to close in for the kill.

Otherwise, hope there is someone around with a rifle to shoot it when you turn to run—a handgun will not be much use as the kinetic energy from such a small gun is not enough to stop a large animal. Much the same advice applies to brown grizzly bears in North America as these enormous animals can run faster than a Thoroughbred racehorse over short distances.

Large bears run faster than racehorses and are adept tree climbers.

REALITY CHECK

When filming *Fitzcarraldo* in Brazil, Werner Herzog's senior cameraman was bitten by a poisonous snake. The locals said he had minutes to live. "Luckily for him," said the famous director, "we sawed off his foot with a chainsaw; otherwise he would not be with us now and the film would not be so good."

Snakes, spiders and scorpions, even relatively small ones, should be considered poisonous and therefore dangerous. In flood situations, every living thing makes for the high ground, including, of course, snakes. In Balochistan, it was almost impossible to walk along a raised embankment above the flood waters without stepping on one. They were everywhere—which is why venom antiserum is such an important component of the emergency medical response. If you see a snake, **back slowly away**. Avoid being bitten in the first place by **wearing heavy climbing boots**.

When sleeping, lie under a tucked-in mosquito net. And make sure you **shake your clothes and shoes** when you get up in the morning before putting them on.

If you do get bitten, radical action as in the "reality check" above is unlikely to be necessary. You will need to react fast, though. First, **compress the limb that was bitten to reduce blood flow** and make it harder for the blood to circulate by elevating the limb. This will slow the circulation of venom. There is nothing to be gained by cutting the site of the bite or using ice.

> A bite from a poisonous animal is a medical emergency.

Only then **suck the venom out of the wound** using a mechanical device (you should have one in your medical kit—see Appendix). If using your mouth, **spit out whatever you manage to extract frequently**, as the venom can enter the bloodstream orally. Since it is already in your bloodstream, you have little to lose. Friends, however, should not expose themselves to this risk.

REALITY CHECK

Dave is allergic to bee stings. Driving through the Australian outback with his twelve-year-old daughter, he was stung by a bee on his thumb. Squeezing the thumb tightly, he extracted the sting with his fingernails and drove back to the nearest road. He knew that stopping a passing car was his only chance of survival, as he had lost his emergency Adrenalin auto-injector and the nearest medical facility was two hours' drive to the west.

Fortunately for him, the first car that passed had what was needed: not an auto-injector—who has one of those lying around on the backseat of their car?—but two bottles of eye drops. It is a little-known fact that, when consumed, some types of eye drops used for hay fever contain enough antihistamine to act as an antidote to a bee sting. And that is exactly what he did, to the astonishment of his daughter and the unwitting benefactor. Apparently, it tastes disgusting!

He didn't know, though, that such drops also contain a chemical that sends you to sleep. He woke some hours later in the hospital, his daughter having driven him there. Some kid—she hadn't even learned to drive!

5

As anyone who has worked in the honey-producing area of South Sudan will confirm, **bees** get angry. African honey bees are three or four times larger than their northern cousins and multiple stings have been known to kill. They are at their most aggressive when the colony is building a new hive—usually in the spring or after the long rainy season.

If attacked by a swarm, **run away—through bushes preferably—and get indoors if you can.** Usually, swarms give up once you have put a couple of hundred yards between yourself and the hive. The trouble is, you have probably been running toward another colony busy preparing *their* hive, and they will have been alerted to your approach by the noise of the chasing swarm and begin to swarm themselves.

Be prepared to run for some time. Flapping wildly only makes them more angry and therefore more likely to sting. Jumping into water does not always deter them, as the swarm often remains hovering overhead. And anyway, there may be something larger—with teeth—in the water.

If stung, **remove the barb carefully with long fingernails or tweezers**. Do not squeeze the sac on the end, as this will increase the amount of venom injected. Unlike the sting of a wasp or hornet, a bee sting remains attached to the venom sac. This can continue to pump venom into the victim for up to ten minutes, so **early and careful removal of the stinger is advised**.

REALITY CHECK

Being confronted by a pack of snarling, slavering, possibly rabid dogs is not a pleasant experience and best avoided. I had been in postgenocide Kigali, the capital of Rwanda, for only a few days when such a pack happened upon me. Luckily, the car was close by, so as the growling animals advanced menacingly, hackles raised, I was able to back up to the car door and slide in.

That night, there was an unusual amount of gunfire echoing through the city. It turned out that the Rwandan army had realized that not only was rabies spreading like wildfire but also the many dogs roaming the streets, surrounded as they recently had been by dead human bodies, had got a taste for human flesh. So they shot them all.

If you are threatened by one or more dogs, **keep your arms by your sides and don't make any sudden movements. Avoid eye contact**, for in such situations dogs interpret eye contact as an aggressive act; staring each other down is what dogs do when preparing to defend territory.

Say nothing, and back away slowly. Turning your back and running triggers the dogs' hunting reflex and almost guarantees you will be attacked. If you are attacked and cannot put some solid protection between you and the dog(s), **climb a tree or get on top of a car** if you can. You can always shout for help from there, and dogs will usually slink away when outnumbered by advancing humans.

> **Avoid eye contact with a snarling dog and back away slowly.**

If all else fails, do the following:

> Use any object at hand to defend yourself. A thick stick is best, but a bag or even a book will do. The attacking dog will try for your throat first. Try to get it to bite the stick, bag or book instead of you.

> If you have a stick, use it to **hit the dog as hard as you can on its nose**. Shove the stick down its throat if the opportunity arises as that will disorient the dog for a while.

> If this has failed to deter the attack, **use your arms to cover your face by clasping your hands behind your neck and pressing your elbows against your nose**. Try to remain standing. But if you have been knocked to the ground, keep your arms where they are and curl up into a ball by drawing your knees into your chest. Keep as still as you can. The dog or dogs will most likely be going for your arms, but that is better than them going for your head or neck.

> **Do not attempt to pull your arm out of a dog's mouth** as this will only result in further injury. Instead, if the dog has your arm in its teeth, push back into its mouth—this makes a dog instinctively open its jaws.

At this point, you have to hope that others come to your rescue or that the dogs get distracted and wander off. Either way, **act like a rock and don't make any sudden movements**.

Once in the clear, clean any wound as best you can with soap and water—remembering that fizzy drinks, beer or urine can be just as

7

good (see **deep wounds** section)—and **seek immediate medical attention**. It must be assumed that rabies is present, so demand treatment accordingly, along with an anti-tetanus booster.

Some of the more "gung-ho" advice on dealing with such an attack suggests it is possible to incapacitate any offending animal by grabbing its forelegs and suddenly wrenching them violently apart sideways. Supposedly this drives the breastbone into the dog's heart, killing it instantly. I am, however, assured that only the strongest of men have sufficient strength to do this to larger dogs. You would have to be in a pretty desperate situation to try it, that's for sure.

> **Dogs can't climb, so get onto something high, like a car roof.**

If you are going for any length of time to a country where rabies is prevalent, **make sure your rabies jabs are up-to-date** before you go (see **vaccinations** section).

... **getting lost**

REALITY CHECK

I was conducting a "rapid health assessment" in eastern Chad, one of the most desolate places on earth, at the beginning of the Darfur crisis in 2004, when we got completely lost. One minute we were following a scrubby track of sorts; the next we had no idea where we were. Once we had admitted defeat and acknowledged our predicament, we oriented ourselves (using one of the methods outlined below) and set off deliberately northeastward, sure that we would cross a road running east–west somewhere to our north. It worked. Because we had deliberately "aimed off," when we hit the road (itself only a sandy track and easily missed), we knew we had to turn left (west). We arrived in the town of Goz Beida as darkness was falling. A simple tale with a successful outcome, but very alarming at the time. Such a seemingly innocuous event often turns into a drama lasting days.

Whether grappling with a map in a moving car or out walking on a windblown hillside, most of us will have experienced that gut-sliding sensation when denial that there is anything amiss turns with growing dread into an awful realization that we are no longer just "temporarily embarrassed as to our location" (as helicopter pilots like to say when hovering near road signs to find out where they are) but utterly and helplessly lost.

If you have no global positioning system (GPS) handset to guide you, the only way to find out where you are—and therefore which direction to travel in to get you where you want to be—is to orient yourself using the sun or the stars, and then **move in a straight line** in a chosen direction until you either recognize a geographic feature or can relate what you see to a map.

The first thing to do is **orient yourself and the map in the same direction** so that you are both facing due north. The gridlines on the map run north–south and east–west, with north at the top of the map as you read it. This is not always "true north," as "magnetic north" can be different by as much as 11 degrees, depending on where you are in the world.

At night, orient yourself by identifying the North Star. Despite what many people think, Polaris— the North Star—is not the brightest star in the sky; in fact, it's the forty-eighth brightest star. What makes Polaris important is that it stands directly above the earth's North Pole, and during the night, all stars appear to revolve around it. From the Ursa Major constellation (the one that looks like a saucepan or hand-plow when the dots are joined up), extend an imaginary line connecting the two stars at the end of its bowl (or plow-share) upward. There, about five times as far away as the separation of these two stars, you'll find one small star that appears brighter than those around it. This is Polaris.

In the southern hemisphere, you will probably not be able to see the Plow. So, instead, identify the Southern Cross constellation and mentally extend a line down from the long arm. To the left are two distinct stars known as the Pointer Sisters. Extend a line perpendicularly down from between them until it bisects the first line as shown in the diagram (left). This point will always be directly above south.

By day, place a 3-foot stick vertically in the ground and mark with a stone where the tip of the shadow falls. This will be point A. Wait for an hour, and place another stone where the tip of the shadow now falls. This will be point B. Draw a line in the dirt between the two stones. This is your west–east line, with A being west. Standing on the line with the stick behind you, you will be facing north.

You can use a wristwatch as a rudimentary compass too. Make sure it is set to local time. With the watch horizontal, aim the hour hand at the sun. Then divide the angle between the direction of the hour hand and the twelve-o'clock position on the watch face, and the line that makes is the north–south line, with north between the V of the two hands of the watch. In the southern hemisphere, point the twelve-o'clock position at the sun, and the midpoint between twelve and the hour hand will give you the north–south line, again with north between the V.

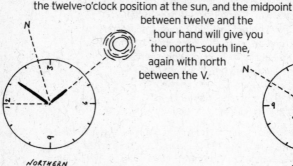

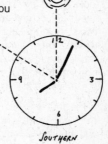

NORTHERN   SOUTHERN

Although not quite so accurate, an imaginary line drawn between the two points of a crescent moon and extended down to the horizon will give you an approximate idea of where south is when in the northern hemisphere—and of where north is when in the southern hemisphere.

In temperate wooded climates, you can get a clue from the local flora, as it is true that moss and lichens tend to grow better on the northern side of rocks and trees. This is because they thrive with less sunlight.

Once you decide to move (it might be best to stay where you are and await rescue), **fix a point on the horizon and move toward it**. But be careful to **read the scale of the map**, as the place you are attempting to reach might be either farther away or closer than you think. This is easier said than done in flat, featureless areas, but there is usually something on which to focus. If visibility is poor, it is best not to move until you can see some distance. Make sure you **measure the distance traveled**. It takes approximately 100 "full" paces to cover 100 yards. The best way to keep count is to use eighteen small pebbles and transfer them one at a time to the other hand at each 100 steps. When all eighteen are in the other hand, you will have covered 1 mile. At this point, pass the job to someone else, then pick up a stone and put it in your pocket. Do this every mile and the total number of stones collected will tell you the total distance you have traveled.

Nowadays, aid workers conducting assessments and humanitarian operations in remote places will have a Thuraya or Iridium handheld satellite telephone with them. Those with more experience will also have a global positioning system device (GPS). The GPS is a satellite-based, radio navigational system. It consists of a constellation of twenty-four active satellites, each of which transmits data that interfaces with the GPS receiver to provide precise position and time to the user. The GPS is not only accurate but, unlike the compass, when set on navigation mode it will guide the user to a selected destination point by actually telling the user how far left or right the user has drifted from the desired heading.

When using these devices to "fix" a current location—for the purpose of plotting the location of a refugee camp or earthquake-affected village, for example—it is important to ensure that the same datum is being used by everyone. Otherwise, the geographic information systems (GIS) mappers will find it difficult to accurately plot the location and ascribe the correct Place Code (P-Code) for use by others later. Because the earth is round—in fact, it is not a perfect sphere but an egg-shaped oblate ellipsoid—something called the Mercator projection is used to transfer a curved surface to a flat piece of paper. There are different ways of doing this, which is why the datum becomes important.

The values of latitude and longitude for a particular position are calculated using a set of imaginary lines covering the earth's surface that, when overlaid, form a grid. Any position within this grid is given a coordinate.

Latitude and longitude are measured in degrees, minutes and seconds, with 60 seconds in each minute and 60 minutes in each degree. These are denoted by the symbols °, ′ and ″. For example, the U.S. Capitol is located at 38°53′23″N, 77°00′27″W (38 degrees, 53 minutes and 23 seconds north of the equator and 77 degrees, zero minutes and 27 seconds west of the zero meridian).

When looking at a map, latitude lines run horizontally and longitude lines run vertically. Latitude lines are also known as parallels, since they are parallel and are an equal distance from each other. Each degree of latitude is approximately 69.2 miles apart, with each minute being approximately 1.15 miles apart (this makes the circumference of the planet roughly 25,000 miles, and the radius roughly 4,000 miles). Degrees of latitude are numbered from 0 to 90 north and south. Zero degrees is the equator, the imaginary line that divides our planet into the northern and southern hemispheres; 90° north is the North Pole and 90° south is the South Pole.

A topographical map will be overlaid with grid lines. The lines will have two-digit numbers against them in the margins. Any point within one of these grid squares is given a series of numbers that is called a grid reference. The numbers going from left to right are called "eastings," and the numbers going from bottom to top are called "northings" (even in the southern hemisphere).

If lost far from human habitation, embarrassing as it may seem, **if you have a radio, use it to alert others** to your plight.

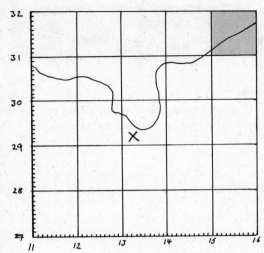

Use the numbers on the grid lines and apply the eastings first. On a 1:25,000 scale map, where each box is one square kilometer, the shaded area shown would be 1531. To be more accurate, mentally subdivide the square into 100 smaller squares of 100 square meters each. The X would therefore be 132292.

Stay with your vehicle. Burning tires are easy to spot from above (but let the air out first or it will explode). Setting tires alight is not so easy. The best way is to set a "Benghazi burner" into a hollow beneath the tire (actually, the whole wheel) and lay the tire over it. A Benghazi burner is a tin can or metal drum two-thirds filled with sand soaked in diesel fuel or gas with air holes poked into the sides near the bottom. If you have a GPS device or satellite telephone, plot your position on a blank piece of paper, having first drawn the eastings and northings. Then plot the position of the nearest known place (all remote UN locations now have their GPS coordinates written underneath the place name) and draw a line between the two. Orient yourself and your rudimentary chart to the north, and then consider as a group whether to move off in that direction or not.

If you are in the desert and do decide to move, **do so at night and keep to high ground**. If you abandon your vehicle, **leave a clue as to which direction you have gone**. An immovable arrow made of sticks or stones cannot be mistaken, and, if it is big enough, may even be seen from the air. As in the "reality check" on page 8, **deliberately "aim off"** so that when you hit a line feature such as a road, river or railway line, you are sure you have to turn in one direction. Many

Aim to miss your objective on one side, then you'll know which way to turn when crossing a line feature.

people die in the desert not far from their objective because they just missed their target and didn't know which way to turn.

When resting, stay in the shade and lie on a camp bed or improvised equivalent at least one foot above the ground—sand and rock can be up to 20º hotter than the surrounding air because of radiated heat.

Breathe through your nose rather than your mouth as much as possible, and **keep clothes on** as this extends the period of sweat evaporation. This is why desert nomads are well swathed in flowing robes.

... lack of water

If traveling in areas where water is of suspect quality, **carry a handheld water filter**. This device can transform the dirtiest, foulest stagnant water to being drinkable in moments. It filters out bacteria and rotavirus, as well as solid contaminants (as long as the ceramic filter is clean). If you don't have such a high-tech filter, the **water must be chemically treated or boiled**. If absolutely desperate, it is always possible to drink the water from a vehicle's radiator (though, even in hot countries, it may have antifreeze in it so it should be distilled first—see page 16).

> **Always boil, distill or add chlorine to suspect water.**

The best places to look for water are at the base of rocky outcrops, up to 6 feet below the surface on the outside bend of a dry riverbed or near clumps of trees.

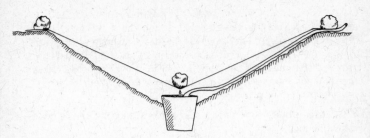

In very dry areas, you may need to construct a "solar still" to condense water from damp or urine-soaked soil:

> Build your solar still in the lowest, dampest area you can find.
> Dig a large hole in the ground, at least 2 feet deep and 3 feet in diameter. The idea is to dig down to damp soil.
> Place a container, centered, in the bottom of the hole.
> Cover the hole with a large (3 feet × 3 feet) plastic sheet. Use the dirt from the hole to weight the plastic surrounding the hole, so that no air can escape.
> Use a small rock to weight down the center of the plastic over your cup, creating an inverted cone with the tip pointing into the cup. As the sun heats up the soil, moisture evaporates and condenses on the plastic. This condensed moisture drips down to the lowest part of the plastic and then drips off into your cup.
> In very dry areas, green (nonpoisonous) plants, damp forest litter and urine can be added to your hole to dampen it. Dig deeper and wider in drier areas.
> If you insert a tube, you don't have to dismantle the still every time you want a drink.

In grassy upland areas, collecting dew just before the sun rises can give you enough water for a few hours. Just tie towels or T-shirts around your ankles, walk through the wet vegetation and wring out the sodden material over a cup.

In very hot climates, or at high altitudes with little cloud cover, contaminated water can be purified using radiated heat, infrared and ultraviolet radiation from the sun. Fill a large (1 liter) plastic bottle two-thirds full of the "dirty" water. Blacken one side of the bottle and

15

place this side down on corrugated iron sheeting or similar reflective material. Leave undisturbed for twenty-four hours. In this time, biomatter (e.g., fecal bacteria) will oxidize and solid matter will settle, leaving relatively clear and drinkable water. This exercise should only be repeated three times before thoroughly cleaning the bottle. I have seen this done successfully in the Altiplano of Peru, where villagers have racks of such bottles lying on their roofs.

If the water is brackish or salty, it will need distilling. This can be done with urine too.

> Get a metal pan with a lid. Remove the lid and place an empty cup in the center of the pan.

> Slowly pour the salty water—or urine—into the pan, stopping well before the level rises to the lip of the cup (you don't want your precious distilled water being contaminated with splashes from boiling salty water, let alone urine). Depending on the weight of the cup, you may need to place some form of weight, a smooth stone for example, into the cup to stop it floating.

> Place the pot cover upside down over the pot so that the highest point or handle is facing down above the center of the cup.

> Bring the liquid to a slow boil. Once boiling, the steam will condense on the underside of the upturned lid, forming water droplets that will dribble down to fall off the lowest point, i.e., into the cup. The boiling will leave all salts behind in the pot.

> It speeds up the condensation process if the lid is kept as cool as possible. To do this, fill the upturned lid with the next batch of water, replacing it when it has warmed up.

If faced with having to melt snow for drinking water, choose ice instead as this takes half as much heat for the same volume of water. (It also prevents "hot spots" occurring, which can wreck the pan.)

If you are without water, the chances are that you are somewhere very hot and also without sunglasses. If so, **prevent sunblindness by covering the eyes with a strip of material into which have been cut a couple of slits** to see through. The same applies in snow conditions where "snow blindness," caused by reflected sunlight, can strike in a single day. The effect may become permanent if some form of protection from the ultraviolet radiation is not afforded.

... **attracting passing aircraft**

Burn a car tire (see **getting lost** section) **and make smoke signals with a blanket.** This is the one Hollywood trick that actually works—those searching for you will realize that the far-off smoke is not an accident but something that should be investigated, whatever the signals do or don't say.

Flash the aircraft by **reflecting sunlight off a mirror** or concave bottom of an empty drink can (having first polished this with a toothpaste-and-charcoal mix). Estimate the angle between the sun and the plane and hold the mirror in such a way as to bisect that angle.

Much of the guesswork can be taken out of this by getting someone else to stand facing you in dark glasses. Direct them to move left or right and to tell you when the mirror is "flashing" them. When they are being flashed and are at the same time standing directly below the plane, tilt the mirror up and down rhythmically. As with smoke signals, this will tell an alert pilot that the reflection is intentional.

Construct as large an X as you can with material that contrasts as much as possible with the surrounding ground. Or a triangle. According to the international air-to-ground code, the triangle informs a (helicopter) pilot that it is safe to land, whereas an X says "a doctor is needed." Don't worry about these niceties; either will do.

> The aircraft that spots you will circle or waggle its wings to confirm it has seen you.

17

... **preparation of landing sites**

In Burundi, in 1995, a UN refugee campsite architect and I designed and built a laterite "dirt" strip for C-130 Hercules emergency airlift operations in three days. . . . It now has a control tower and a sign saying "Welcome to Ngozi International Airport."

It became clear that such a strip was needed when the roads were washed away during the previous rainy season, and with them any chance of feeding the growing number of Rwandan refugees and displaced Burundians who were congregating on the outskirts of this tiny town. The polo-playing architect had never taken on such a task before, but he was the only person available with any kind of engineering qualifications. I became his partner on the even more questionable basis that I was the only person within the relief community who had ever had a pilot's license. The fact that it had expired some ten years earlier, and was in any case for flying small helicopters rather than large fixed-wing transport aircraft, was not enough of a disqualification.

Time was of the essence. The two of us drove into the remote Burundian highlands to make a reconnaissance of the likely sites and begin discussions with village elders and landowners about ownership and access—this, in itself, was a not uneventful journey as it involved negotiating numerous roadblocks set up by the heavily armed and suspicious Hutu rebels who roamed the country at that time. Using the morally dubious argument that construction of such a landing strip would catapult the sleepy little town of Ngozi into a major international travel and trading hub, we secured the necessary assurances and began work. We paced the scrub, stuck wet fingers in the air to test prevailing wind direction, and worked out on the back of an old exercise book what was needed. Three days later, with the help of over 1,000 volunteer laborers, 200 borrowed shovels and 1 tractor-trailer, we had our strip. The orientation, diagonally across the narrow valley, was slightly unorthodox—a compromise to avoid a river, unhelpful crosswinds and two steep and wooded hills on either side.

Leaving instructions for how to make smoke on hearing the noise of approaching aircraft engines, I set off back to the capital, Bujumbura, to see if I could find and persuade an old bush pilot to attempt the first landing. Two days later, a wonderful French former Mirage (fast jet) pilot called Jean-Luc, myself, a couple of intrepid UN national staff (neither of whom had flown before) and a few bags of food aid "buzzed" the newly constructed strip in a Twin Otter, a solidly built all-purpose aircraft used by bush pilots across Africa. Jean-Luc made three low passes before landing, with his head out of the window to get a better look at our handiwork. At the second pass, cattle and goats grazing next to the runway could be seen galloping off in all directions, chased frantically by their young and equally panicked herders. As we sideslipped in for our final approach, I could see hundreds and hundreds of people running down the hill toward us. As we bumped and lurched down the runway, our hearts in our mouths, black oily smoke momentarily obliterated our vision—the keen young watchman had been a bit overzealous with the diesel-fueled "Benghazi burner"—but at least Jean-Luc had been able to factor in his crosswind component. We jolted to a jubilant stop well before the end of the runway. Jean-Luc turned the aircraft, switched off the engines and climbed down. "Well, how did you find it?" I asked nervously, for I felt personally about this project. "*Ça va*," he replied. "A bit more grading to smooth the surface, perhaps. But long enough, wide enough and clear of obstructions."

Drawing deeply and deliberately on a filterless Gitane, he added nonchalantly, "Although I think we should cut down some of the trees on the approach path." With this, he leaned down to remove a branch from the landing gear.

Less than one week later, Belgian air force C-130s were flying twelve sorties a day into this strip.

Ten years later, I helped Pathan villagers in Pakistan's North-West Frontier Province recover from the devastating earthquake of October 2005 by showing them how to build helicopter landing sites (helipads) among their steeply terraced rice paddies. After a short "training of trainers" program, villagers could construct a stone helipad, complete with windsock and a painted *H*, in approximately six hours.

Helicopters will fly at night in the case of a medical emergency but are very unlikely to land at the pickup point unless (a) they have **established (VHF) radio communications** with the ground party and (b) **the landing site is properly illuminated and clear of obstruction.**

Final approach will be slower and steeper than usual—this is more dangerous in the event of engine failure but safer in terms of the higher risk of hitting a previously unseen obstruction. Remember, it is difficult for a pilot to see wire—even more so at night.

Clear helicopter landing sites of anything not heavy or fixed.

For all landings, first determine whether the area is large enough to land a helicopter safely. The landing surface should be flat, firm and cleared of debris that could blow up into the rotor system. The *H* usually seen in the middle of permanent helipads is not necessary for temporary versions used in field operations. However, should you wish to include one, make sure it is painted and does not consist of material, even if that material is pegged or weighed down with rocks. If rotor downwash gets under any such material, it is likely to scatter rocks, pegs and the material itself in all directions—an event most pilots, even Ukranian bush pilots, would prefer to avoid.

Any slope should not be more than 6°. The touch-down area should be a minimum of 100 feet x 100 feet (30 m x 30 m) during the day and 150 feet x 150 feet (45 m x 45 m) at night for an Mi-8 or smaller.

At night, ensure that spotlights, floodlights, flashlights or flares used to define the area are not pointed toward the helicopter. Turn off non-essential lights.

Park two vehicles 30 feet (10 m) apart downwind of the intended landing site, facing slightly in toward each other with headlights

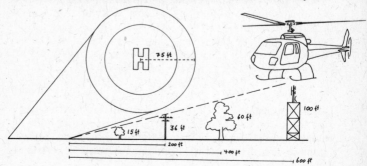

on full beam pointing into wind. The intended landing site is where the two beams intersect. If the vehicles are fitted with Codan HF radios, **make sure the antennae are removed.**

One person should help guide the aircraft to a safe landing. That person must wear eye protection, as helicopters throw up a lot of sand and grit when slowing their descent to land. (S)he should **stand at the upwind edge of the landing site with back to the wind and arms raised overhead**, indicating the landing direction.

If the helicopter is depositing an under-slung load, **do not touch either the net or the cable attaching it to the aircraft (the "strop") until it has touched the ground**.

"Grounding" discharges enormous amounts of static electricity that have built up in flight. Touching the load without first allowing for this is likely to result in you becoming the conductor of what is, in effect, a bolt of lightning—which can kill you. A British RAF ground handler forgot to do this in Muzzafarabad in Pakistan during the earthquake relief operation and was hurled across the tarmac by the discharge from a Chinook. Luckily, he survived.

Allow under-slung loads to "ground" before touching them.

Fixed-wing operations should be designed with the C-130 Hercules in mind, although most logistical lifts will actually use smaller aircraft such as the Transall or Twin Otter.

For the C-130, runway length should be 1,500 yards (1,400 m) if possible, although short landings with reduced fuel and payload (6 tons) and experienced bush pilots can be done in three-quarters of this distance. However, taking off becomes something of a lottery with such a short runway; much depends on wind speed and direction, runway conditions, slope, temperature and altitude. Runway width should be 100 feet across, including a 10-foot cleared "shoulder" on either side. An additional area, termed the "clear zone," of 100 feet around the sides and ends of the strip must be cleared of trees and shrubs.

It is not necessary for the landing strip to be perfectly level, but it is important that gradient changes are not sudden. Embedded rocks, sharp stones and any lumps of soil of more than 10 centimeters across must be removed. Ensure that there are no ditches or significant holes (more than 10 cm deep or across) between the strip and the clear zone. Fill them in if there are.

The grade should slope from the center (at an angle of no more than 2°) to allow rain to run off. Orientation should be into prevailing wind unless there is an obvious obstruction such as a hill or radio tower in the way. Turning circles are needed at both ends, and a parking area is required for loading/off-loading. The wingspan of a C-130 is 132 feet and it has a turning circle of 140 feet (based on the aircraft center-line).

Before unleashing the bulldozers, make sure you have permission of the landowner and/or village elders. As in the "reality check" on pages 18–19, once the benefits of an airport to the community have been pointed out, objections are rare. However, animals of all sorts and sizes continue to wander around as local farmers negotiate compensation for upset grazing rights.

Livestock is a constant hazard to pilots. The pilot will often make a low pass down the length of the runway to check its condition and to scare off any animals grazing nearby before commencing his/her final approach. Help the pilot by shooing away any animals grazing nearby when you hear the aircraft approaching. If the site is newly in use, it is important to **assign ten men to guard the plane once it has come to a stop**. They should carry sticks and be briefed to prevent unauthorized approach, especially by children, and to stop any smoking in the vicinity. If it is a helicopter that has landed, they must make sure no one approaches from behind, as anyone walking into the tail rotor will be very efficiently decapitated.

It is helpful to the pilot to **make some smoke** so that (s)he can tell the wind speed and direction.

Inspect the strip by driving down it 10 minutes before the arrival or departure of an aircraft.

If an emergency landing at night is needed, put lights (flashlights pointing toward the incoming aircraft are suitable) at 15-foot intervals along the threshold, i.e., at the downwind end of the runway, and place burners at regular (150-foot) intervals down at least one side, but both if you have enough lights. If using "Benghazi burners," try to ensure that smoke does not obscure the runway.

A few drums of aviation fuel (usually Avgas or Jet-A1) may need to be stored on site. Keep them under lock and key, if so. Be careful not to dent or break the seals on the drums, as the fuel is hydroscopic and is easily contaminated with water as well as dirt. Store the drums on their sides, with seals at the three-o'clock or nine-o'clock position. Before using a drum of fuel, stand it upright for at least one hour to allow any water or sediment to settle. Refuel with a hand

A "Benghazi burner" is a tin can or metal drum filled with sand soaked in diesel fuel or gas.

pump, as improvised gravity-fed systems can be dangerous. You may have noticed that pilots do not take unnecessary risks, and especially fear fuel problems in flight. They are likely to reject any fuel that appears to have been badly handled, which may have implications for takeoff payload—you may be the one left behind.

For passengers, the check-in desk at such dirt strips can usually be found under the nearest large tree.

... flying without a pilot

REALITY CHECK

It is not unknown for pilots to pass out on the job, or get shot. Even though there are normally two, you may find yourself flying in the "right hand" (co-pilot's) seat one day, as I did in North Darfur. We had finished a long day's negotiation with the SPLM rebels and a helicopter from the African Union was due to pick us up. We knew it was coming when the rebel soldiers squatting under the tree scattered in every direction without warning—we had certainly not heard anything. They were understandably suspicious of everything airborne, since the appearance of aircraft overhead was usually accompanied by the dropping of bombs.

As soon as the helicopter had found us (we had had the foresight to take along a couple of bright green smoke grenades), landed and closed down, one of the pilots got out and promptly threw up all over the wheel. He was clearly not fit to fly. As is often the case in humanitarian operations nowadays, the pilots were Ukrainian and spoke neither English nor French. With what I could remember of my limited Serbo-Croat, I managed to tell the captain that I had once been a military helicopter pilot and could help him fly back to his base at El Fasher. What I did not tell him was that I had been trained only on small four-seat Gazelle helicopters and had never flown a large 28-seater transport helicopter—let alone one with instrument readings in Russian. To the surprise—and, they later told me, consternation of my colleagues—he let me help and between us we managed to fly home safely, with me, it has to be said, only "following through" on the controls. But at least I helped with the navigation.

Once you have taken over as pilot, fly straight and level while taking instructions from the air traffic controller over the radio. **Get someone else up front with you**, even if only to **read out these instructions**. Remind yourself that a good emergency landing in bad terrain can be

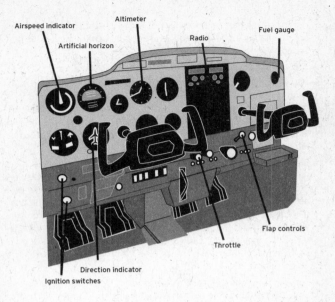

Airspeed indicator
Altimeter
Artificial horizon
Radio
Fuel gauge
Flap controls
Throttle
Direction indicator
Ignition switches

less dangerous than an uncontrolled landing on an established airfield. You will end up doing the following:

> Drag the pilot out of his seat, take his place and grab the controls (or "yoke"). Pull to go up. Push to go down. Rotate left to go left. And rotate right to go right. Maintain the aircraft in straight and level flight. Rest your feet on the pedals but don't bother using them until you are ready to land.

> Identify the flight instruments one by one, including the throttle, flaps and landing gear levers (see illustration above). Work out where you are, which direction you are flying in and at what height.

> Put on the headset and call "Mayday" three times while pressing the transmit button on top of the yoke. Be prepared to answer using the aircraft's call sign, which can be found written on the dashboard. If you get no response after three attempts, change to the emergency frequency 121.5 MHz. The person in the control tower who answers you will then "talk you down" to land at the nearest airfield.

> If you get no answer, then you will have to land yourself. Look

25

out for a likely field (reasonably flat, without obstructions, and approximately 1 mile in length) and descend toward it by reducing speed.

> If the wheels are not fixed, lower the landing gear.

> You will want to land into wind. There are usually visual clues as to wind strength and direction, such as smoke and wind patterns in grassy fields. Use them and orient yourself to be flying downwind (i.e., with the wind behind you) so that the right wing-tip is over the chosen landing point as you pass 1,000 feet. Turn right about two minutes later and keep turning until the runway is ahead of you.

> Line up on the runway or intended landing field and maintain 70 knots of airspeed. Vary your rate of descent using the throttle. If you are confident, engage 15° of flap. If not, ignore them. Try to fly down an imaginary "glideslope," using only foot pedals for direction and throttle to control rate of descent. Push the left pedal, and the plane will yaw left, and the same with the right. The plane will slowly line up with the center-line but will remain straight and level while doing so. Using the pedals will increase your rate of descent, though, so be prepared to use more throttle.

> The aim is to stall the plane as you drift above the runway a few feet above the ground. The aircraft will stall at approximately 55 knots, so don't go any slower than that during your approach.

> Once the wheels touch the ground, push hard on the tips of both foot pedals. This will engage the brakes, which are used for steering the plane on the ground.

There are over fifty different electrical and mechanical devices on the panel in front of the pilot. Ignore all of them except the ones described in the following table, as these are the minimum you need in an emergency situation—and if *you* are flying, it *is* an emergency situation. Identify each in turn and, when flying straight and level a few thousand feet above the ground, get the feel for what each one does by practicing. Tell your (frightened) passengers what you are about to do before you do it, as this will increase their confidence.

Airspeed indicator	Tells you how fast you are flying through the air. Because of wind, this is *not* the same as speed over the ground. Do not drop below 60 mph.

Direction indicator	Works like a compass and tells you in which direction the plane is heading.
Artificial horizon	Tells you the "attitude" of the plane. Keep the horizontal white bar aligned with the blue/brown line to fly straight and level.
Altimeter	This tells you your altitude. Because air pressure changes, this is *not* the same as your height above the ground.
Radio	Don't change frequency unless you hear nothing. Turn the knob to change frequency (121.5 MHz is the universal emergency frequency). The transmit button is on top of the steering column.
Flap controls	These control the flaps for landing. Set the lever to 15° when on final approach. The aircraft will slow down and point slightly higher. From now on, use the throttle to adjust your rate of descent.
Throttle	Pull the knob out, or push the lever between the seats, to go faster.
Control column	Rotate it to the left and the aircraft will turn left. Likewise to the right. Pull to go up. Push to go down. It's that simple. Be firm but gentle.
Trim wheel	Rotate it until the pressure on the control column neutralizes.
Fuel gauge	Land within 15 minutes when the needle goes into the red.
Ignition switch	To start the engine, turn the key.
Master switch	This turns on all the electrical devices in the aircraft. You can't start the engines until this is done.

Continued on next page >

Landing gear	There will be one of these only if the undercarriage is retractable. On final approach, depress the lever until three green lights show or the knob turns from red to green. The aircraft will slow appreciably, so be prepared to add more power.
Pedals	You don't really need the pedals until lined up on the final approach to the landing strip. The plane will fly perfectly well without them. You need them on the ground, however, to steer and to stop. Push the tips of both at the same time to brake.

I don't know anyone without a pilot's license who has had to start up, taxi and take off in a single-engined light aircraft—if it's twin-engined, you *have* got problems—but I can think of places where it could become a possibility. Dirt strips in Puntland, Somalia, for example. It's actually quite straightforward—this is what you have to do:

> Strap in to the left-hand seat, put the headset on and place your feet on the pedals. Ask someone sensible to do the same in the right-hand seat.

> Turn on the electrical ignition switch (just a normal switch marked "ignition"), wait 30 seconds for all the whirring and clicking to calm down (it's just the instruments orienting themselves) and start the engine by turning the key—just like a car.

> With the doors firmly shut, open the throttle slowly. This is either a knob on the dashboard that you pull or a lever between the seats that you push. Steer the aircraft along the ground using the tips of the pedals. Push with your left foot and the aircraft will slew left, and vice versa. Push both at the same time to brake.

> Line up at the end of the runway into the wind (this is important, so make sure you know the wind direction before starting up) and, when everyone is ready, open the throttle all the way quickly and firmly.

> Steer down the runway using the pedals. These move the tail fin and will become progressively more responsive as you accelerate. Hold the yoke (steering column) in a centered but neutral position, i.e., don't force it.

> There is an obvious moment when the aircraft wants to take off. When you notice this, gently and firmly pull the yoke a few inches (10 cm) toward you without twisting it.

> Once airborne, and if you're feeling smart, push the lever marked "Wheels" to retract the undercarriage and throttle back to 75 percent power (75 percent engine noise), and then carry on as described above. Easy, really.

... **helicopters**

Unlike fixed-wing aircraft, helicopters are inherently unstable. You will not be able to fly one, let alone land one, therefore, without specific training. The best you can do if you do find yourself in one of the front seats is to **make a semicontrolled "crash landing" onto water**, as you will surely crash catastrophically if attempting this on land. At least the water will stop the rotor blades and prevent explosion, even though passengers will have to swim out of a machine that is not only sinking but also turning upside down (because most of the weight—the engine and gearbox—is on the top).

For the record, there are three controls, one for each axis of movement: the "cyclic" controls the pitch (angle of attack) of each individual rotor-blade cyclically. This is the stick between the pilot's knees, and it controls movements sideways,

> **Any landing from which you walk away is a good landing.**

forward and backward. The "collective" controls rotor pitch collectively, i.e., all rotor-blades change pitch at the same time. This is the lever that looks like the handbrake in a car. If pulled up, the helicopter lifts, and vice versa. The foot pedals control the tail rotor, and therefore the yaw of the helicopter. So far, so good. The problem, however, is that an input into any one of these three controls affects the other two because of something called "torque," which tries to twist the helicopter.

There are also minor details such as "inflow roll," "transverse flow" and "gyroscopic precession" to compound the challenge of controlling torque, any one of which will cause the helicopter to crash if not carefully and constantly controlled by the pilot. Compared to flying a plane, control inputs are minimal as the helicopter is a very sensitive machine. Overall, this is why military people refer to helicopters as "50,000 rivets flying in approximate formation." UN pilots go further by adding ". . . and put together by the lowest-cost bidder."

29

The humanitarian world uses helicopters a lot, for the simple reason that those worst affected by natural disaster—normally the poorest and most marginalized—live in inaccessible places and have been cut off from the outside world. Roads have been rendered impassable by earthquake damage, washed away by mudslides or submerged, or the bridges destroyed by floodwater.

The **Mi-8** is the workhorse of humanitarian operations. It carries up to 4.5 tons of freight internally (2.8 tons under-slung), with the major advantage that loading is possible through clam-shell doors at the back, and can accommodate up to twenty-four passengers. It can be found operating in the mountains of Pakistan, the Sahel sands of Darfur and the steamy littoral of Liberia. Partly this is because, being of the Soviet era, they are robust. But mostly, having been chartered from the lowest bidder (Ukraine), it is because they are cheap.

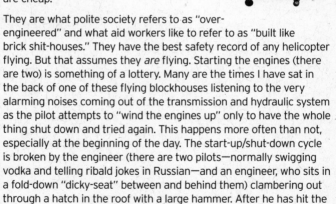

They are what polite society refers to as "over-engineered" and what aid workers like to refer to as "built like brick shit-houses." They have the best safety record of any helicopter flying. But that assumes they *are* flying. Starting the engines (there are two) is something of a lottery. Many are the times I have sat in the back of one of these flying blockhouses listening to the very alarming noises coming out of the transmission and hydraulic system as the pilot attempts to "wind the engines up" only to have the whole thing shut down and tried again. This happens more often than not, especially at the beginning of the day. The start-up/shut-down cycle is broken by the engineer (there are two pilots—normally swigging vodka and telling ribald jokes in Russian—and an engineer, who sits in a fold-down "dicky-seat" between and behind them) clambering out through a hatch in the roof with a large hammer. After he has hit the turbine injectors hard twice, the engines usually start.

Once airborne, these machines have the added advantage for passengers of portholelike round windows that can be opened so far that it is possible to lean out. With hot exhaust gases vented through the leading edge of the rotor blades, they also fly safely in very cold, icy conditions that ground all western helicopters. The avionics (dials), however, are not only labeled in Russian (and read backward) but are also frequently not working.

With a crew of four and able to carry up to 100 people or 22 tons of cargo, the **Mi-26** is the largest helicopter in the world. During earthquake-relief operations in Pakistan in 2005 and 2006—when over 150 helicopters from twenty-six nations were involved in air-lifting aid to remote high-altitude locations—the use of this helicopter was limited to dropping under-slung loads only because the downdraft from its eight rotor blades would blow away the roofs of entire villages. I watched one aid drop where over fifty villagers were sent tumbling down a steep mountainside, unable to stand against the windstorm this beast kicked up.

The **Chinook** (CH-43) helicopter is obvious because of its twin-rotor configuration, with the rear set higher than the forward set so they can't hit each other. These two sets of blades contra-rotate (i.e., one set goes clockwise, the other counterclockwise), which means that there is no need to divert power to a tail rotor. Consequently, despite its relatively small size when compared to the Mi-26, it can lift 14 tons or up to fifty-five passengers (but only thirty-three troops, who tend to have more stuff attached to themselves . . . like guns and ammunition).

Like most NATO helicopters, it is, however, what one pilot I spoke to described as "a little temperamental." In other words, it breaks down a lot. Out of the six RAF Chinooks operating in Pakistan for earthquake-relief operations, only three could ever be relied upon to be "on the flightline" at any one time. The record of the American Chinook fleet was even more dismal. On top of that, NATO pilots are more risk-averse than their Russian or Ukrainian counterparts, who appear to have never heard of "health and safety"—or, for that matter, "don't drink and drive." As a result, these "workhorses of the sky" were frequently grounded by bad weather (which didn't stop the Ukrainians from flying, of course). Rumor has it that the RAF have had to deliberately "ground" their aircraft in conditions they deem flyable when their American counterparts won't fly in order not to embarrass their "more emotionally fragile cousins." But there again, having had to rely on the RAF to extract me from patrols before, I suspect that the truth could be the other way around.

The **Puma** is smaller than the other cargo carriers mentioned here, and is used almost exclusively by the International Committee of the Red Cross (ICRC). Painted white with a large red cross, these machines can carry eighteen people or six stretcher cases. Hardly a sortie goes by without some form of technical problem occurring. Once, flying out of Bosnia toward the Dalmatian coast, I used my best French to persuade the captain to let me have a "cabby" in the co-pilot's seat. I was just clambering over the engineer to get in when there was a double hydraulic failure. The instrument panel lit up like a Christmas tree and alarms began to sound in the cockpit. I was grabbed by the co-pilot, who had just vacated his seat, and thrown bodily into the back of the aircraft. We made a "precautionary" landing, as the flying manual suggests one does, poured some more hydraulic fluid into the system and took off again. We landed in Split—at the Royal Naval Air Station base temporarily established there and officially called "RNAS Banana, Split" (quite true)—twenty minutes later, where the captain later explained to me that such systems failures were "*absolutement normale*" for the Puma.

Also, being French built, the Puma's rotor system goes the other way to everybody else's, which means that they require the opposite control inputs. You cannot therefore fly one type of helicopter and then just climb into a Puma and expect to be able to fly it. That is why, I suspect, they are not used much.

In the Asia-Pacific region, it is common to see what look like pre-Wright Brothers light helicopters such as the **Llama**. For the most part, these are used for VIP visits and medical evacuation. Don't be discouraged by their rather outdated appearance, however, as these machines have rescued mountaineers off Everest when no other helicopter could get to them.

In conflict zones such as Afghanistan, helicopter gunships can frequently be seen flying at extremely low level. It is as well to know which type belongs to whom, as to be inadvertently on the receiving

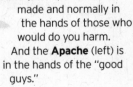

end of one of these—as too many aid workers have been—can "bring tears to the eyes." The **Hind** (above) is Russian-made and normally in the hands of those who would do you harm. And the **Apache** (left) is in the hands of the "good guys."

... firing an AK-47

The only protection afforded an aid worker is his or her neutrality. That is why aid workers must not bear arms. However, in an increasingly dangerous world, where the distinctions between civilian, soldier and humanitarian have become blurred in some conflict zones, there may come a time when you have to defend yourself. This actually happened during the attack on the UN guesthouse in Kabul in October 2009. More likely, there may come a time when you need to shoot an animal some distance away for food.

In these scenarios, the weapon available will probably be the AK-47, otherwise known as the Kalashnikov, after its Russian inventor. The reason these weapons are to be found the world over is that they don't jam, even with minimal maintenance. They can be seen all over Africa with up to five magazines held together with garish electrical tape.

An AK-47 is both an automatic and semi-automatic weapon. On "automatic," bullets will come out of the barrel for as long as the trigger is pulled (and the magazine has rounds in it), while the semi-automatic setting requires a separate trigger pull for each bullet fired.

Load by inserting a full magazine of up to thirty rounds into the obvious space underneath the barrel. Unload by depressing the magazine catch. The magazine catch is located between the magazine and the trigger guard. Make sure the selector switch on the right is in the up position. Grasp the bolt catch (the little piece of metal protruding from the bolt). Pull the bolt sharply backward until it will go no further, and release. You now have a loaded rifle, so exercise caution by not pointing it at anybody.

There is a selector (or safety) switch on the right side of the rifle. It is a thin piece of metal that protrudes from the right and moves up and down. When the selector switch is in the down position, the rifle is in the semi-automatic fire position. When the selector switch is in the mid position, the rifle is set for automatic fire. And when in the up position, the rifle is on the safe setting and cannot be fired. The "click" is very distinctive on an AK-47. Make sure that anyone carrying a gun anywhere near you has set it to "safe." This is particularly important when armed guards are in the same vehicle as you (which you should try to avoid by having them travel in a separate vehicle), especially if the road is bumpy.

For shooting, set the rear sight to the range required. Grasp the firearm with one hand (overhand) on the hand guard and the other hand on the pistol grip or stock, with the index finger resting outside the trigger guard. Raise the weapon and pull the stock firmly into the right shoulder. (If you use the left, hot brass cartridge cases will be ejected at speed into your face.) Aim by aligning the target with both front and rear sights. Move the selector to the automatic or semi-automatic position when ready to fire. Maintaining a steady aim, place your index finger on the trigger and squeeze gently until the trigger releases the hammer. To fire a second round when set to semi-automatic, you must release the trigger and repeat. If set to automatic, maintain a firm overhand grip on the barrel and push down hard as the rifle increasingly tries to "climb" high and right.

... **tying knots**

It is surprising how many people attempt to tie boats to jetties, plastic sheets to poles, or cars to one another for towing without knowing how to tie safe knots that (a) don't come undone, and (b) can be undone after intense strain. Here are some of the basics:

The **bowline** (pronounced "bow-lin") makes a fixed loop at the end of a rope. This can be particularly useful when joining two ropes together. It is also easily undone after being under extreme tension. The technique for tying this knot is best remembered by "the rabbit comes out of the hole, goes around the tree and then back down the hole."

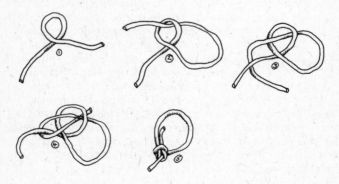

The **reef knot** ties together two ropes of different thicknesses. It is also the best knot for tying together bedsheets (see **escaping a burning building** section). The normal mistake is to make the same half-knot twice—which creates a granny knot that slips when under tension. The top half is the opposite to the bottom half. Think of the string rather than your hands. The same string goes from left to right, over, under and over again. Then it returns from right to left, over, under and over again. You must be careful when tightening the knot. Pull both strings equally and not too hard at first. If you pull one string much harder than the other, the knot will be pulled out of shape, and at worst will be merely a number of loops of one string round the other.

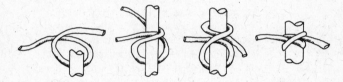

The **clove hitch** fixes rope around branches or poles and can be tensioned. It is useful when fixing plastic sheets making emergency shelters to ground pegs. It's also what sailors use to tie up boats. A clove hitch is made by making a loop in the rope (with right over left), then another, and then passing the right-hand one under the left-hand one and slipping the two loops over a (mooring) post.

The **trucker's hitch** is what logisticians and drivers use to tie down heavy loads. An eye is formed by twisting the rope, after which a loop is passed through the eye. The purchase is then created by passing the free end around the hook on the truck and then back through the loop. After tightening, the tail is used to tie two half-hitches below the original loop.

... using the radio

Two vehicles traveling in convoy in the desolate Jebel Moon area of West Darfur were held up at gunpoint by a group of Janjaweed militia, who were at that time carrying out a campaign of ethnic cleansing and wanted to discourage internationals working for aid agencies from witnessing their atrocities. The occupants were robbed, beaten, stripped naked and left in the desert with a little water while the militiamen drove off in their hijacked vehicles. The temperature was over 115°F, and they had no shade. Life expectancy in such conditions is measured in hours. Less than one hour later, a UN helicopter rescued them. All six lives were saved that day by the quick thinking of the Sudanese driver in the lead vehicle, who, knowing that if he were seen using the radio he would be shot on the spot, discreetly pressed the "emergency cell-call" button on the handheld radio clipped on his belt, out of sight of the now-close militiamen. This alerted the UN radio operator back at base that something was amiss and he could listen in real time to the hijacking as it unfolded while the militiamen remained unaware that their actions had been "spotted." He was also able to pinpoint their location to within one square mile by triangulating the signal from multiple radio-relay masts in the area. The helicopter pilot who rescued them later said that, had they moved, his crew would probably not have spotted them in the rock-strewn vastness.

Good communications are vital to safety and security when conducting humanitarian operations in the field. Where networks are available, mobile phones are the medium of choice. In really remote areas, satellite telephones will be needed. Both of these are backed up by radios. Aid workers operating in conflict zones plan resupply over the radio, regularly update their location by radio, receive evacuation instructions over the radio and conduct regular radio checks to confirm their safety—including one at the end of the day to check safe arrival at home before curfew. For similar reasons, drivers will inform the (UN) radio room when departing and arriving. They will also give regular radio checks along the route. In short, the radio becomes your best friend. Know how to use one, and get used to having a VHF handheld clipped to your belt.

Very high frequency (VHF) radios work more or less on line of sight, which limits their range to approximately 10 miles for a handheld and 50 miles for one mounted in a vehicle. This depends on the power of the transmitter, the terrain (the higher the better) and whether or not the antenna is vertical—which it should be (angled antennae reduce performance by up to 75 percent). Weather affects performance only marginally. As a rule of thumb, don't rely on VHF communications once the distance between stations exceeds 25 miles or so. For longer distances, high frequency (HF) radio is used, which is why such radios are fitted in vehicles when VHF repeaters are not available. Because they use a much longer wavelength, weather has a major effect on their performance. Motorola appears to be the manufacturer of choice for VHF, while Codan seems to have captured the UN market for HF.

If you are using solar panels to recharge the batteries, make sure these remain clean and oriented toward the sun. If the length of cable connecting the panel to the battery is longer than 25 feet, the cable must be at least ¼ inch in width and well insulated, or significant loss of power will result due to resistance. If even 10 percent of the cells on the solar panel are in shade or covered in dust, output can drop by 25 percent or more. This is because individual cells become resistors rather than capacitors.

Nowadays, VHF handheld radios offer a digital selective call encoding facility (Selcall) that causes the selected receiving radio (or radios) to ring like a telephone even if the volume is turned down (which it will be if you are sleeping with it next to you). When you are talking, it operates like any other radio transmission, but the advantage is that the caller does not have to call everybody just to talk to one person— especially useful at night when "traffic" is low.

The facility has one other major advantage: when used in conjunction with the little red emergency button on the top, all preprogrammed numbers will automatically hear what is going on around you while the radio itself appears to be inert. This has proved itself a life-saving technology during attempted robberies and carjackings, as the base station is not only alerted to your predicament but can also triangulate to find out where you are. **If you are in trouble, press the red button.** If it is pressed by mistake, remove the battery as this will reset the facility. In some countries, pressing this button alerts all the emergency services, including the military, which means they take your safety very seriously.

For most VHF users, it is enough to know how to change the battery, turn the radio on and off, what frequency to select (these have been precoded so it's just a matter of turning a knob to select a number), which button to push to transmit and what to say when transmitting. It's this last bit that gets people nervous, as they know the whole world is listening. **Know your call sign** and those of your colleagues you are most likely to call. (In Burundi, the UN security officer's radio call sign was "Whisky Six Zero." He would be introduced in person as "Whisky," rather than by his real name. He even started calling himself "Whisky," and his wife still does.) After that, **think what you want to say in as few words as possible before pressing the transmit button**, then use radio procedure as follows:

> Busy radio networks have a designated "calling channel" and others for passing messages. Sometimes, one of these will be dedicated to particular subgroups of, say, NGOs. Establish contact with the call sign you want to speak to, and then transfer to the agreed channel.

> Before transmitting, wait until there is a pause in the traffic and then **press the transmit button half a second before speaking**, as this allows the electrical relays to activate. If there is an emergency, however, transmit immediately preceding your message with "break, break." Everybody else will then shut up.

> The originator of the call begins by saying "hello" and the call sign of the station he wants to talk to, followed by "this is" and his own call sign.

> Every transmission should end with the word "over." It is then up to the receiver to respond. Do not say "over" and then continue talking.

> When the call has been completed, the final transmission will end with the word "out." "Over and out" is unnecessary if you think about it. If the call has not finished but more than a few seconds are needed to find the answer to a question posed by the caller, suspend the call with the words "stand by."

> If you have understood what is being said to you, the formal reply is "roger." However, users nowadays more normally use "good copy."

Phonetic Alphabet

A	Alpha	J	Juliet	S	Sierra
B	Bravo	K	Kilo	T	Tango
C	Charlie	L	Lima	U	Uniform
D	Delta	M	Mike	V	Victor
E	Echo	N	November	W	Whisky
F	Foxtrot	O	Oscar	X	X-Ray
G	Golf	P	Papa	Y	Yankee
H	Hotel	Q	Quebec	Z	Zulu
I	India/Italy	R	Romeo		

Numbers

Transmit numbers by pronouncing each digit separately as follows:

10 = One Zero

18.75 = One Eight Decimal Seven Five

2,300 = Two Three Zero Zero

5,000 = Five Thousand

Standard Words and Phrases

Acknowledge	Let me know you have received and understood this message.
Affirmative	Yes.
Break	I am interrupting with an urgent message. Stay off the air.

Continued on next page >

Five by five	I hear you perfectly (four being less clear, down to one, which is almost unintelligible).
I say again	I repeat for clarity or emphasis.
Loud and clear	Your signal and readability are excellent.
Mayday	Emergency. All others stay off the air.
Negative	No.
Nothing heard	I cannot hear you at all.
Over	My transmission is ended and I await a response.
Out	Transmission is ended and no response is expected.
Roger	I have understood your message. "Good copy" is also used.
Say again	Repeat your message.
Stand by	I will call back.
Standing by	I am waiting for you to call back.
Unworkable	I can hear you transmit but cannot understand you.
Wait one	I will check and call you back (used most often by the military). The "one" refers to the one minute this is supposed to take.
Weak	I hear you with difficulty.
Wilco	I understand your message and "will comply" (not used much now).
Wrong	No, you have misunderstood.

In theaters of humanitarian operation, call signs are allocated by the controlling "base" station, usually the UN's Department for Security and Safety (UNDSS), according to the nomenclature outlined below. You cannot just make up your own.

The first letter of your call sign refers to where you are based; the second refers to the agency you work for; the third is a number designating your role within the organization; and the fourth is also a number, which indicates your level of seniority. Sometimes, drivers add a fifth (normally "alpha") to indicate that they are answering on their passenger's behalf.

Second letters correspond to the following UN agencies:

A	Food and Agricultural Organization (FAO)
B	World Bank
C	UN Children's Fund (UNICEF)
D	UN Development Programme (UNDP)
E	UN Cultural Organization (UNESCO)
F	World Food Programme (WFP)
H	World Health Organization (WHO)
L	UN Joint Logistics Center (UNJLC)
M	International Organization for Migration (IOM)
N	UN Population Fund (UNFPA)
O	UN Office for Coordination of Humanitarian Affairs (OCHA)
P	UN Operations and Programme Services (UNOPS)
Q	UN Department of Peacekeeping Operations (DPKO)
R	UN High Commissioner for Refugees (UNHCR)
S	UN Department for Safety and Security (UNDSS)
T	UN Human Settlements Programme (UN-Habitat)

Continued on next page >

U	UN Secretariat
X	for NGOs
Y	for NGOs
Z	for NGOs

These numbers refer to the position within the agency:

1	Management and miscellaneous senior staff
2	Finance/administration
3	Logistics
4	Program
5	Staff security/guards
6	Agency specific
7	Drivers
8	Technical support staff, e.g., telecoms, IT, etc.
9	Visitors/agency specific

So, for example, my call sign when visiting Dushanbe in Tajikistan as a consultant for UNICEF was "Delta Charlie Nine Two" where D = Dushanbe, C = UNICEF, Nine = visitor, Two = the second visitor in-country at the time (and I kept this call sign even after the first visitor had left).

... **feeling good**

As I was often told at the beginning of my military training, "Any fool can be uncomfortable." But discomfort wears you down over time and renders you less able to do your job. It also irritates those around you who have bothered to look after themselves and are suitably prepared. The following are tips on how to remain reasonably comfortable against the odds:

> Keep warm and dry in cold climates by using multiple (no more than three) layers of thin clothing underneath one thermal outer "shell" jacket. The layer next to the skin can be woven from natural or man-made fiber, but it must be "wicking" (i.e., constructed using modern technology that "wicks" away sweat). Wear thin cotton outer pants with roughly woven thermal leggings underneath. This combination dries faster than any other.

> Wear two pairs of socks, no more: one thin pair next to your skin and one pair of thick thermals. If they get wet, remove them, squeeze them dry and place them under your armpits while plunging your (cold, white, wrinkled) feet into the nearest stream—the colder the better. After two minutes, dry your feet and replace your socks, making sure that those originally on the left foot are now on the right. This changes the tread pattern of the fibers and ensures good circulation. Replace your boots (having remembered to tip out excess water) and walk briskly. Your feet will be toasty warm in a few minutes.

> In hot climates, use a rimmed hat with built-in neck-and-shoulder protection, not a baseball cap.

> Make sure you have a universal bath plug in your toilet kit as these are something of a rarity in low-income countries.

> Keep twenty squares of toilet paper in a resealable plastic bag in your hip pocket.

> Wear a small flashlight and multitool on your belt at all times.

> Carry a small bottle of Tabasco (or something similarly spicy) and a packet of vegetable and/or chicken stock cubes in your backpack.

> Have fruit-flavored oral rehydration salts (ORS) in your medical kit.

> Use 50 percent DEET insect repellent in the evenings while wearing long trousers and long sleeves (roll-on is best; use sparingly on wrists, back of hands, temples, forehead, back of neck and ankles; and be aware that concentrations above 50 percent can melt plastic).

45

> Sleep in a sleeping-bag liner (preferably silk) and use a cotton pillowcase. Use eyeshades and earplugs if in a shared space where people come and go all night. Use a camp bed rather than a compressed foam mattress on the floor if you can.

> Pack a (vacuum-packed) emergency rain poncho.

> Create some personal space with your own music selection on an MP-3 player.

... looking good

Neither gel nor foam nor soap is necessary for shaving; any form of oil will do, and actually gives a closer shave while not irritating the skin. Oil with menthol negates the need for aftershave, too.

Unwanted hair can be (painfully) removed by "threading." Twist half a dozen threads together and roll them quickly up and down the area in need of depilation. The hairs will snag between the threads and be torn out of the follicles.

On R&R (rest and recuperation), it is accepted that women will immediately gravitate to the nearest "spa" so that, if only for a few hours, they can imagine they are being pampered somewhere warmer and friendlier. But, if isolated from such necessities for too long, there are "field" remedies for those needing a lift:

> For a facial, smear the face with warm honey and scrape off after thirty minutes with a blunt knife. The honey can be mixed with oatmeal—a great natural exfoliant—if you wish. Note that the "goo" can be eaten afterward!

> To de-wrinkle after overexposure to the sun, apply tea-tree oil, rehydrate by drinking plenty of water and cool the skin with aloe vera.

> To de-bag under the eyes, place cucumber slices or old, cold teabags over the eyes for thirty minutes (close eyes first).

> For lipstick, use Vaseline or oil with a hint of brick dust mixed in.

> To condition hair, rinse after washing with an egg yolk. Henna is also good, when available locally, although if you don't want it to give your hair a strong red sheen, mix it into natural yogurt first. And don't leave it in for too long, i.e., no more than fifteen minutes.

Many ambassadors invite their nationals at least once a year to an embassy "do"—even those who have been buried in deep-field for months. For these occasional brushes with civilization, men always need a tie and a dark-colored crumple-proof jacket somewhere in their luggage. There is no need for anything more fancy.

The equivalent for women is the "little black dress" (or longer variant if in an Islamic country), and the superelegant always seem to find space for some high heels. If the dress's hem comes down, fix with a stapler or tape and burn off loose threads with a cigarette lighter. If wearing tights, ladders can be stopped with a dab of nail polish or soap. Broken heels can be fixed with superglue and/or a nail driven in from the top and bent over at the bottom. If all else fails, break off the other heel. And scuff marks can be covered with ink from a felt-tip pen.

Chapter 2

Health and Hygiene

How to deal with...

Looking after yourself in remote places is a priority. Many of us take our health for granted but quickly find that what would be a minor inconvenience at home escalates into a health emergency when away. Tropical medicine requires a different set of treatments from those we are used to. Seemingly insignificant cuts can turn into infected wounds that fester for weeks, and what might pass for "*la grippe*" elsewhere just might be malaria or dengue. As ever, prevention is better than cure. Don't allow yourself to ingest contaminated water. But if you have been exposed to what doctors like to call "enteric pathogens," take the situation seriously and prevent dehydration by drinking liters and liters of oral rehydration salts (ORS)—not just plain water. Minimize the risk of getting bitten by bugs, especially mosquitoes, by wearing long-sleeved shirts and pants in the evening.

This section takes you through the more obvious aspects of first aid, not all of which are orthodox. It also deals with the kinds of injuries found in disaster zones, war zones and in bomb-blast sites, as, hopefully, you will have had little exposure to these at home.

REALITY CHECK

I had left to go on holiday the day before and my office was empty when the UN Canal Hotel office complex in Baghdad was blown up by a truck bomb in August 2003. I was lucky, but twenty-two of my friends and colleagues were not and died that day—eighteen of them from injuries related to flying glass. Many more were injured.

When dealing with multiple casualties, a decision has to be made about whom to treat first. This process is called "triage." Ignore those making a lot of noise at first and concentrate on the motionless bodies. These are the priorities in which first aid should be given:

> Check for breathing and pulse
> Control bleeding
> Cool burns
> Splint fractures
> Treat shock

Remember there is a risk of cross-infection when giving first aid to a patient where bodily fluids may be transmitted. If possible, wear disposable gloves or even plastic bags. Otherwise, cover any of your own cuts or wounds with a bandage before administering treatment to someone who is bleeding. **Wash your hands carefully before and after treatment.** You can use some form of dry-wash or a baby wipe.

You must always be vaccinated against tuberculosis, hepatitis A and B, meningococcal meningitis, typhoid, diphtheria, tetanus, poliomyelitis and yellow fever prior to deployment. It is not advisable to attempt to be vaccinated for more than three of these at any one time; develop a vaccination (booster) schedule with your doctor well before departure (see **vaccinations** section).

Personal medical kits and trauma kits in vehicles are usually found lacking in field situations. Aid workers are exposed for long periods in situations where decent medical care might be some days away. Every medical tip that follows has been carried out by aid workers in the recent past. A list of personal medical supplies required by all aid workers when in the field can be found at the back of this book.

If you don't need some of the things it lists, one of your colleagues surely will.

To check for a pulse, press two middle fingers (not your thumb) firmly against the side of the patient's neck (not the wrist).

If you are not sure whether the patient is breathing or not, hold a mirror to the mouth and check whether condensation forms on the glass.

... **an unconscious person**

If the patient is unconscious, carefully arrange the body into a position that is least likely to do further harm or complicate injuries already sustained. This is called the "recovery position." It is used in order to:

> maintain an open airway
> allow vomit to flow away
> maintain a stable position
> allow the back of the casualty to be examined

Don't leave your patient unattended for more than three minutes.

... **resuscitation**

REALITY CHECK

Following the tragic events that took place in Vukovar at the beginning of the Yugoslav Wars in 1991, a wounded Serb nurse was bundled unconscious into the back of a military truck and driven to the nearest hospital in Novi Sad—a nighttime drive over shell-cratered roads that was to take over three hours. Little hope was held out for her survival. At the last moment, a young British doctor working for the World Health Organization leaped aboard. He and an untrained Serb colleague took turns administering artificial resuscitation for all that time, keeping at it until the nurse was safely in the operating room. Thanks to their efforts, she lived. Some fifteen years later, she became the deputy minister of health in Serbia. The doctor, an anonymous hero like so many aid workers facing such situations, went on to found a respected British medical NGO.

If the heart has stopped beating, the patient is in cardiac arrest. You must pump the heart manually in order to get the blood to circulate. To ensure that the blood has oxygen in it, always combine chest compression with artificial ventilation. External cardiac compression with artificial ventilation is known as cardio-pulmonary resuscitation (CPR).

> Move the patient on to his or her back on a firm surface, *unless* there has been injury to the head, spine or neck.

> With one hand, find the patient's lowest rib, sliding your finger to the point where the ribs meet the breastbone. Place your middle finger over this point and your index finger just above it. Place the heel of your other hand above your two fingers. This is the area where you will be applying pressure.

> Place the heel of your first hand on top of the hand that is now correctly positioned and interlock your fingers.

> Keeping your arms straight, lean forward and press down on the sternum (breastbone) until it is depressed about 2 inches.

> Remove your hands and allow the chest wall to spring back. Repeat this at a smooth, regular rate (80 compressions per minute) for

15 compressions. Stop the compressions, give six breaths of mouth-to-mouth ventilation and repeat.

> For mouth-to-mouth ventilation, tilt the head back, hold the jaw open, pinch the nostrils, physically check the airway is clear with your fingers, take a deep breath, place your mouth over the patient's and blow firmly (less so for a child, and even less so for a baby). It takes more effort than you might think to inflate the lungs of an adult.

> Continue this cycle until the pulse obviously returns. Don't waste time rechecking for breathing or circulation unless there is an obvious sign of life (breathing or movement).

> If you feel a pulse, stop compression immediately but continue with artificial ventilation until the patient is breathing on his or her own.

If you are in a remote situation without easy access to more advanced medical support and a pulse has not returned, the reality is that the patient will probably not survive. In these circumstances, resuscitation should be discontinued after a maximum of one hour. CPR is hard work. Take turns if you can.

... choking

Choking on a foreign body is a common cause of death. Because of this, all restaurants in New York are obliged to display a poster explaining the Heimlich maneuver. This maneuver is easy to do and is a lifesaver. Most of us know someone who has performed it.

Sometimes food or, in the case of a child, a small toy or a hard candy gets into the back of the throat or even into the trachea and can't be expelled by the normal epiglottal reflexes. The Heimlich maneuver forces the foreign body up and out of the airway by driving a sudden burst of air from the lungs. If an adult is choking, but conscious and standing, ask them to bend forward and cough. If this doesn't work, or they are unable to do it:

> Stand behind them, encircling their abdomen with your arms, halfway between the belly button and the ribcage.

> Make a fist, positioning your thumb to their stomach just below the breastbone.

> Grab your fist with your other hand and with a short, sharp thrust press upward and inward into the stomach.

> Repeat as required to remove the object.

Turn small children upside down and shake them by their feet instead, as the Heimlich maneuver will break their ribs.

If you are on your own and choking, it is possible to perform this maneuver on yourself by violently and suddenly hugging a solid object whose blunt edge is first placed under the breastbone. High-backed chairs and tree stumps have been successfully used in the past.

If all else fails and the patient is unconscious, turning blue and cannot breathe at all—no gasping, no coughing—a tracheotomy is required. This procedure is carried out as follows:

> Find the indentation between the two collarbones and make a horizontal incision about a half inch deep and one inch long with a razor or scalpel one inch above it. There will not be much blood.

> Make a further incision through the tracheal tube. This is made of cartilage so is difficult to cut. Insert your finger into the slit to open it.

> Insert a plastic tube into the hole to a depth of approximately half an inch. The tube can be a hollow pen or medium-size syringe with the pointed end cut off.

> Breathe into the tube with two full breaths, pause and repeat until the patient starts breathing on their own.

... the "runs"

Diarrhea is an occupational hazard and you will not escape its debilitating effects. But you should still minimize the chances of coming down with the "runs" by eating fully cooked food that is still hot, by avoiding ice cream, drinks with ice cubes, and salads and by peeling fruit. Some Dutchmen I know insist that "a bottle a day keeps the doctor away." They are talking about alcohol. And there is some evidence that spirits do indeed mitigate the worst effects.

Drink only water that you know has been boiled or properly treated and use bottled water when brushing your teeth. That said, there is some evidence that limited exposure to local pathogens actually increases individual resistance to the more virulent bacteria. That explains why some field workers insist on using tap water when brushing their teeth. But spit it out, don't drink it.

Acute diarrhea is usually self-limiting and therefore not life-threatening. But it is temporarily completely incapacitating. If suffering from the "runs," make sure to maintain your fluid levels by **drinking one large glass of oral rehydration salts (ORS) per visit to the toilet**. You should always have at least six packs of (preferably flavored) ORS in your medical kit. If you run out, make up your own by mixing eight level teaspoons of sugar with one level teaspoon of salt in one liter of clean water.

I have met people in the field who swear by the curative effect of cola taken at room temperature without the bubbles (take them out by shaking). Eating plain rice, yogurt or bananas helps too.

Take two Imodium tablets at onset, then one every four hours. Some people prefer charcoal, either as tablets or in its "raw" form. **If there is blood in your stools, stop the Imodium and instead take 500 mg. of co-trimoxazole.** This is an antibiotic that cures the majority of cases of diarrhea. If your symptoms are severe and persistent, you are vomiting or if you have dysentery (i.e., vomiting or passing blood, fever), take 500 mg. every day for five days and rehydrate with 4 liters of ORS per day. You should be seeing a doctor if it has come to this.

... **delivering a baby**

REALITY CHECK

Women have been giving birth since the beginning of time without much help, so don't try to do too much. When more than one million Rwandan refugees returned en masse from the refugee camps in Eastern Congo, groups of women could be seen from time to time at the side of the road helping a new mother give birth. Amazingly, such groups had nearly always moved on within a couple of hours.

If the baby is oriented with its head up and feet or buttocks showing first (a breech delivery), renew your efforts to get help quickly—preferably from a midwife or traditional birth attendant (not necessarily a doctor). Today, breech babies are usually delivered by Cesarean section, a surgical procedure that you will not be capable of performing. There is nothing you can do—do not attempt to push the baby back into the womb, for example—so continue with the delivery as outlined below if you can.

Talk to the woman. Tell her to breathe. If she feels like pushing, encourage her to pant rather than breathe between efforts. Have her push when contractions are strong and rest at other times. Do this until the contractions are strong and the baby's head is emerging (crowning). This happens much faster in countries where mothers are used to "home birthing" than in more developed countries.

Cup the baby's head in your hands once it starts to come out and move it slightly downward as the woman pushes. **If the umbilical cord is wrapped around the baby's head or neck, gently work it free.** Help the shoulders to ease out one at a time. Once both shoulders are clear, the baby will slip right out in something of a rush. The baby is very slippery and easy to drop as a result. It will be slimy and covered in what looks like white cream (vernix). Don't wipe this off. Instead, wipe the baby's face with a towel and **check that the nose and mouth are free of obstruction**.

Even in warm climates, hypothermia is a major cause of unnecessary neonatal death. To prevent this, pat the baby dry, place it so that it has skin-to-skin contact with its mother and then cover both with dry, clean blankets.

If the baby is a bright navy-blue color or, if it is a dark-skinned baby, its lips are bright blue, rub its chest gently but firmly. The chances are it will soon return to its normal color.

Do not cut the umbilical cord. Instead, tie it as tight as you can with a single string or shoelace approximately 6 inches from the baby. In developed countries, two plastic clamps are used, and the cord is cut between the two. In an emergency, just the one clamp will suffice.

Do not try to pull the placenta out; it will come out on its own up to two hours after the birth. **Only cut the cord once the placenta is out.** Do this on the mother's side of the knot you made earlier. Leaving the cord intact helps increase the baby's iron levels, which reduces the risk of anemia.

People are sometimes surprised at how large the placenta can be; often it is as large as the baby itself. It, and the umbilical cord to which it is attached, often pulse for a while after parturition.

The baby might excrete soon after birth. Don't be surprised when you see that the feces are black. Don't be shocked at the shape of the baby's head either; it can be almost conical at birth—such is the pressure in the birth canal—but soon regains its normal rounded shape.

The greatest cause of maternal mortality is postpartum hemorrhage after giving birth. In most cases, **blood flow can be stopped by pressing a clenched fist hard into the woman's stomach just above the pubic bone**. Very firm abdominal massage can have the same effect as this helps the uterus contract after delivery. But both techniques assume the placenta is out. Do this until the bleeding has stopped, and for a few minutes afterward. These simple techniques have probably saved more mothers' lives in this situation than any other through the years.

... **inserting a catheter**

Shock is a condition caused by a sudden decrease in the volume of fluid in the body's blood circulatory system. This condition can be fatal. In the absence of a trained medic, aid workers must be prepared to initiate an intravenous infusion (IV) to add fluid to the patient's circulatory system. The sooner the patient receives IV fluids (basically a solution of various salts and/or electrolytes added to water; Ringer's is the one most usually found in such situations), the more rapid the improvement in condition. Red Cross delegates are trained in IV insertion, whereas the military tend to use anal insertion (just the tube without the needle), as this is easier and more effective—the colon is the most efficient part of the gut for water absorption.

The golden rule of IV therapy is to use the largest vein and the smallest-gauge catheter possible. The cephalic and basilic veins in the forearm are preferred. These will stand out once you begin the steps outlined below (which you should get someone to read to you).

Just to make you feel less inadequate, "grab and stab" and "hope and poke" are terms nurses use to describe IV catheter-insertion techniques. Most have not received formal training but learned "on the job."

> Place a constricting band (a belt will do) around the patient's arm 6 to 8 inches above the selected infusion site.

> Tell the patient, if conscious, to clench and relax their fist several times and then to keep the fist clenched. If the patient is unconscious, place the limb below the level of the heart. Gently tap over the vein at least ten times.

> Clean the skin with a sterile swab or alcohol beginning at the site and spiraling outward.

> Remove the unit from its protective packaging.

> Place the thumb of your nondominant hand about 1 inch below the injection site and over the vein.

> Press on the skin to pull it taut over the injection site.

> Position the needle slightly to the side of the vein at approximately a 20° to 30° angle to the surface of the skin, with the bevel up.

> Insert the bevel into the vein (a slight "give" may be felt) and hold the needle steady.

> Once blood is seen in the flash chamber, advance the catheter/needle unit about ⅛ inch farther to ensure that the catheter itself is in the vein.

> Continue to hold the flash chamber with your dominant hand. Grasp the catheter hub with your other hand and thread the rest of the catheter (not the needle) into the vein (to the hub). Never reinsert the needle back into the catheter.

> While holding the catheter hub with your nondominant hand, use a finger on that hand to press lightly on the skin over the catheter tip.

> Secure the catheter to the skin with tape (go right around the arm if necessary) so that it will not move.

> Remove the flash chamber and needle from the catheter with your dominant hand and put them to one side.

> Tell the patient to unclench their fist.

> Remove the constricting tubing. The constricting band should have been in place for less than two minutes.

> Grasp the adaptor end of the IV tubing with your dominant hand. Remove the protective cap from the adaptor, insert the tip of the adaptor tightly into the hub of the catheter and attach the IV bag.

In Sri Lanka, coconut milk straight out of the king coconut has apparently been successfully used in place of Ringer's lactate (but I don't advise you try it).

... hypothermia and frostbite

Hypothermia can quickly set in with any combination of cold weather, high elevation, strong wind and being wet. The secret is to recognize the danger signs early. Danger signs are feeling intensely cold, shivering, drowsiness, slurred speech and a loss of balance and coordination. If this happens to you or any of your colleagues, **warm up without delay by replacing wet clothing with dry, ensuring that head, hands and feet are covered**.

It is especially important to keep the head covered as significant body heat is lost that way if it is left exposed. **Share bodily warmth with two in a sleeping bag**. Don't be shy. A climbing instructor once told me—but I can find no evidence for this—that young girls between the ages of 10 and 14, teenage boys and menopausal women are more exothermic than the rest of us, i.e., they radiate more heat. Something to do with hormones, perhaps? The inference is that sharing your sleeping bag with a partner from one of these categories raises your chance of survival.

> **More body heat is lost from the head and the wrists than from elsewhere on the body.**

Frostbite is dangerous: you can lose a finger or toe, even an arm or leg, if you don't treat it properly. Do everything in your power to prevent frostbite before it occurs, but **if you see any possible symptoms of frostbite, treat immediately by rewarming the affected area**. Fingers should be warmed by holding them next to the skin—under the armpits is best—rather than blowing on them, which actually cools them as the moisture in your breath condenses and then evaporates.

A Doctors Without Borders doctor I met in Balochistan advised that **taking a large (1,000 mg.) dose of aspirin or ibuprofen** is advisable at this point, as it acts to widen blood vessels and therefore stimulates circulation.

Do not attempt to thaw frozen tissue if it is at risk of being immediately refrozen. It is better to delay thawing for a few hours than do this.

Force the sufferer to **take at least one warm drink. Soup would be best.**

Frostbite is, in simple terms, a freezing of the skin. If it is caught early enough, when it can be reversed, it is referred to as frostnip. Often prone to frostnip are the nose, toes and fingers. The skin will be red and later turn pale. There has been no permanent damage at this point. If frostnip is observed, it is vital to get those spots rewarmed right away so that it doesn't go further and become frostbite. Warm these spots by placing them against warmer skin elsewhere on the body.

When frostnip has progressed to frostbite, the affected skin will be white. It is also very hard to the touch. **Initial treatment is rapid rewarming in lukewarm water**. Slow rewarming when there is a danger of refreezing is not recommended. Do not use water that is hotter than 140°F (60°C) or you risk a burn. **Do not rub or massage frostbitten skin** with snow or anything else as it is being warmed.

The thawing in warm water will take about forty minutes. This may be a painful process. When the skin has returned to red or pink and is once again soft, the thawing is finished.

When the skin has warmed and is no longer numb, **apply dressings to the affected areas, including between the digits**.

Avoid alcohol during this period. **Avoid using frostbitten feet or fingers**, or further damage may be done. **Avoid direct heat** from fires or hot-water bottles.

Multiple layers of thin thermal wear are more effective at retaining body heat than large outer jackets. A "wicking" vest of man-made fiber or silk is best next to the skin. The same applies to socks: wear one thin (wool or cotton) layer and one thicker pair of thermal socks over these. Any more and ridges form in the material, which cut off circulation. When wet, socks should be taken off, wrung out and replaced on the opposite feet. Mittens are better than gloves.

... heatstroke

This condition is life-threatening and the patient's body temperature must be lowered immediately and aggressively. The patient will have hot, dry skin, with a body temperature well above normal. Over 104°F (40°C) is life-threatening while 113°F (45°C) means imminent death. (S)he may be delirious, convulsing or unconscious—symptoms that come on very rapidly. As with suspected heat exhaustion, **get the patient into some shade, remove their clothing, fan vigorously and apply the coldest water-soaked compresses possible. Immersion in cold water is preferable.** Once the patient is conscious, encourage drinking of cold water or rehydration solution.

To avoid heatstroke in the first place, wear a wet bandana around the neck and a wet shirt. If water is scarce, at least keep the pulse points—inside the wrists, the scalp and the temples—cooled by placing wet cloth over them as blood temperature can be lowered by as much as 5°F (3°C) by cooling these areas. If water is not available (from the car radiator, for example), alcohol can be used instead.

... deep wounds

A wound is "deep" if you can see bone and/or tendon. The priority is to minimize the chance of infection before getting the patient to a doctor. In remoter parts of the world, you may be all there is. In which case, you must not only clean the wound but also stitch it. This is neither as awful nor as painful for the patient as it looks—one effect of adrenaline is to dull the pain.

Remove clothing in order to treat the wound. **Don't try to remove an object impaled in the wound** as it may be helping reduce blood loss. **Instead, wrap pads around the wound.**

Clean the wound and surrounding area with a fizzy drink (cola is good), urine, beer, any "white" spirit like vodka, or water (in that order of preference). You must be fairly brutal in this. A can of fizzy drink stings less than alcohol and does just as good a job. Shake the can first and spray it into the wound. You may have to use a few. If urine is used, the donor should be free of any sexually transmitted disease.

Some cultures **pour honey into the wound** after cleaning. Don't discourage this—it acts as a good antiseptic, a barrier to further contamination and is a natural healing agent. If you don't have any honey, **spray or sprinkle the wound thoroughly with a more "Western" antiseptic** such as iodine or hydrogen peroxide powder.

Squeeze together the sides of the wound and hold them together with a sterile dressing. In an emergency, any soft, absorbent pad will do, such as an article of clean clothing, a cotton sanitary pad or tampon.

Apply a bandage over the pad and lift the wounded part above the level of the heart. This reduces blood pressure to the area.

The scalp bleeds profusely. **Use your fingers to press the edges of a scalp wound directly against the skull.** This is better than exerting pressure over a wider area with a pad or the palm of your hand. Use fingertips to stop small squirting blood vessels (arterioles).

If the wound won't stay together, then you should consider stitching as a temporary measure while looking for a doctor. For skin closure, generally a reverse cutting needle is used. This has the cutting edge on the outer curve and is used for tough, difficult-to-penetrate tissues such as skin.

> **Beer, cola and urine are sterile and therefore good for cleaning wounds.**

For suture placement, close and match the wound edges and keep them compressed as they will be under tension. Pierce the skin as far back from the edge as the skin's thickness, then push through using the curve of the needle to reemerge on the other side of the wound the same distance away. Double-tie the suture as tight as you can without puckering the skin. Cut and repeat with no more than half a centimeter between stitches. Sutures should be removed early enough to avoid suture marks but late enough that the wound will not reopen. It is best to reinforce the closure by bandaging.

If the patient goes into shock (pale, faint and sweaty), encourage them to lie down and raise their legs above the level of the heart. A cup of hot, sweet tea (or something similar) is advised at this point.

> **A cup of hot, sweet tea is good for shock.**

... **bullet wounds and mine injuries**

REALITY CHECK

I took shelter with a Spanish TV crew behind a building in Mostar, Bosnia, as bullets were "cracking" down the side street around the corner. We were sharing a cigarette when the cameraman suddenly stepped out without telling us what he was about to do and began to film the scene. Before his soundman could pull him back, he was shot in the lower abdomen just below his bulletproof vest. We dragged him back behind cover. I could hear him telling his friends that he was okay and that it didn't hurt as I scrabbled to unwrap the (military) "first field dressing" that I kept in the pocket of my own flak jacket. I pressed it to the bleeding entry wound as best I could, but it was soaked within seconds. One of his colleagues ripped off his shirt in a further attempt to stem the bleeding. There wasn't much else we could do. Within what seemed moments (but were probably minutes), a white Spanish Battalion ("SpanBat") armored personnel carrier screeched to a halt beside us, but it was too late.

Bleeding is the most common cause of avoidable death. **Most bleeding will stop if firm pressure is applied at the point of injury (for example, by means of a dressing applied over the injury) and/or on the "pressure points" (where the major arteries pass over large bones) and when the affected limb is elevated above the heart.**

Both antitank and antipersonnel mines are set off by vehicles passing over them, whereas antitank mines do not always detonate if (lightly) trodden on. Limbs can be blown off by both, even when in a car (although this is less likely if an antiblast blanket is fitted, or, as in Bosnia, the floor of the vehicle is lined with half-full sandbags). Lives can be saved in such an eventuality by controlling the bleeding. Interestingly, stumps don't bleed that much, as arteries tend to "withdraw" and close up by themselves as a natural reaction to limb loss.

Whatever the cause of such violent injury, **do not attempt to remove any objects (glass, wood, metal) from the wound** itself as this may actually increase blood loss. The victim will be in shock. **Talk to them and keep them talking if you can. Provide as much water or sweet drinks as the patient will take, but avoid alcohol**—this dilates the arteries and veins, promoting blood loss.

If life-threatening bleeding from a limb cannot be controlled by pressure and elevation, improvise a tourniquet as a last resort.

> Do not remove bandages when they become soaked in blood.

Arterial bleeding is obvious, as it spurts rhythmically. In such cases, a tourniquet is most likely to be needed. **Use a piece of rope, or a twisted piece of material (a man's shirtsleeve, for example), with a knot made in the middle and tie loosely above the wound, high up on the thigh or upper arm with the knot over the pressure point**. Insert a stick between the skin and the tourniquet and **rotate until the tourniquet is hard and tight**. There will be an immediate slowing of blood loss. **Release the pressure for 1 minute every 10 minutes, and then reapply** until the patient can be removed to a medical facility.

Gunshot wounds are, along with mine-blast injuries, the most serious forms of trauma you may encounter. Bullets cause three types of trauma:

> penetration (destruction of flesh by the bullet)
> cavitation (damage from the bullet's shock wave in the body)
> fragmentation (caused by the "tumbling" bullet, and/or bone fragments)

It is very difficult to visibly assess the damage done by a bullet, as many internal injuries are likely to have been caused by its passage, even if the entry wound is small and apparently clean. For this reason, the best you can do is stabilize the gunshot victim and get him or her to a hospital.

Controlling the bleeding is the most important thing you can do to save a gunshot victim's life, and applying direct pressure to the wound site is the best way to control bleeding. Use a pad. If you have nothing available, use your hands. But **keep the pressure on**.

Chemical hemostats such as Quickclot® have been proven to be very effective in stemming blood loss. The instructions are as simple as: Hold the wound open, pour in the powder and apply strong sustained pressure.

Gunshot wounds frequently lead to shock, a condition caused by loss of blood that causes reduced blood flow throughout the body. Expect the victim to go into shock and treat him or her accordingly (see **inserting a catheter** section). However, do not elevate the legs if the gunshot wound is to the torso, as this will increase bleeding and make it more difficult for the victim to breathe.

Gunshots to the chest can cause what is known as a "sucking chest wound." Air travels in and out of the wound with each breath, making it difficult for the victim to breathe. In this event, seal the entry wound with some airtight material (e.g., a plastic bag).

... **severed limbs**

REALITY CHECK

In April 2005, a U.S. government official was blown up by a mine in South Darfur. Her lower leg was found a few yards away. Because one of my tasks while working for the World Health Organization had been to establish a medical emergency response team (MERT) in the nearby town of Nyala, a doctor from the Swedish Rescue Services Agency was able to attend and stabilize the patient within half an hour. He retrieved the limb—which, according to the advice elsewhere in this book on what to do in minefields, he probably should not have done—and flew with the patient and the properly cooled limb to Khartoum (a complicated logistics affair involving diversion of an African Union military helicopter and the commandeering of a visiting private jet). Later that same day, she was medically evacuated to Nairobi, where her life was saved and the limb reattached.

With the right micro-vascular, neurological and orthopedic surgical facilities, severed limbs can be successfully reattached. Upper-limb reattachments are more successful than lower-limb procedures, which involve more muscle mass. The extent of damage to the severed limb makes a difference: a sharp or "guillotine" amputation, where there is a clean cut with well-defined edges and localized damage to soft tissue, nerves and blood vessels, is the easiest to repair. Reattachment is least likely to succeed after a crush or tear injury, such as those suffered during explosions, or where there has been significant nerve damage.

Cooling tissue buys time as lower ambient temperatures slow tissue degeneration and substantially increase the time that is safe to elapse between injury and surgery. Typically, limbs must be reattached within six to eight hours, although fingers and toes can be reattached up to twenty-four hours after injury if cooled. **Wrap the severed body part in (clean) plastic bags, insulate with a piece of clothing and place in a (preferably insulated) box full of ice or frozen food**. The idea is to lower the ambient temperature rather than freeze the body part itself.

... broken limbs

REALITY CHECK

In 2007, I fell down a mountain and broke my back while carrying out a health-risk assessment in Pakistan's North-West Frontier Province. It took four hours for the two Kalashnikov-toting Pathan farmers who rescued me to carry me to the nearest road and a further eight hours to get me to the hospital in Islamabad in an old ex-Soviet jeep. It might be something of an understatement to suggest that this was not the most comfortable journey of my life. According to the surgeon who put me back together, the fact that I had not been paralyzed was not a miracle but entirely due to the fact that these two farmers had strapped me tight to an old door.

When I had recovered enough to get back into the field some three months later, I went to find these farming brothers to thank them for rescuing me. I knew they would not accept cash, but despite the extreme poverty in which they lived, they would not accept the windup radio I had bought them either. Nor would their cousins accept an offer to "secretly" buy the family some sacks of rice instead. According to them, helping someone in need without expectation of reward is the spirit of their faith. Either way, it was a humbling experience.

Pain from broken bones can be reduced with splints. You can improvise a splint from any straight piece of wood or metal. Even tightly rolled newspapers are effective.

The form of splinting depends on the site of the fracture, but normally a fractured limb should be firmly strapped to an adjacent healthy part. So, for example, a broken leg should be strapped to the other leg. A broken arm should be strapped to the chest. Broken fingers or toes should be strapped to the next ones.

Lay the splint alongside the suspected break and bind firmly but not too tightly with bandages or lengths of material from ripped-up clothes or blankets. For a lower-arm or wrist fracture, carefully place a folded newspaper, magazine or heavy piece of clothing under the arm. Tie it in place with pieces of cloth. A lower-leg or ankle fracture can be splinted similarly, with a bulky garment or blanket wrapped and secured around the limb. A person with a hip or pelvis fracture should not be moved. If the person must be moved, the legs should be strapped together (with a towel or blanket in between them) and the person gently placed on a board.

... burns

REALITY CHECK

When driving to assess water safety in Bangladesh in the aftermath of Cyclone Sidr, my UNICEF driver suddenly pulled over when he suspected the engine of overheating. Before I could stop him, he undid the radiator cap (not a good idea!) with the result that high-pressure scalding water sprayed all over one of his arms, burning him quite badly.

Villagers quickly crowded around, and one local woman quietly took two eggs out of her wicker basket, broke them and smeared them over the affected area. He found this very "cooling." By the next morning, the blisters, and the pain, had gone!

Tents and naked flames don't mix and should always be avoided. **If a candle is used, it should be placed in a jar or can.** If you inadvertently set fire to yourself, **stop, drop and roll**, as this is the best way to extinguish the flames if there is no nearby body of water in which to submerge yourself.

If burns have been sustained, **remove the victim from the source** and cool the skin. Even when exposed to heat for only a short time, the skin will go on "cooking" if not cooled—just like chicken after it has been removed from the oven. **Pour (clean) cold water over the burned area until such time as the patient feels that the tissue is no longer "cooking."** This may take up to an hour. However, in cases of extensive burns, be careful not to allow the victim's body temperature to drop. A hot, sweet drink should be sipped if possible, as this will mitigate the effects of shock. **Thin plastic wrap (of the type used for sandwiches) is a simple and effective dressing,** but do not wrap the burn tightly and, if wrapping the face, make sure the nose and mouth are left clear. Do not use gauze or other fibrous material as a dressing—individual fibers will stick to the burn and cause disfigurement, if not secondary infection. **Do not cover chemical burns at all, but wash** as above.

All burns can become infected. **Do not break any blisters**, as this may increase the risk of infection. Our skin serves as a barrier against infectious agents and loss of fluid; the more intact it is, the better. **Do not use topical oily applications such as butter**, sometimes advocated by local healers. Although eggs seem to work.

... toothache

Toothache results from an infected cavity. If you have an abscess (a pocket of pus at the tip of the root) your cheeks will be swollen and the infected tooth will hurt like hell when tapped with something metal (the end of a teaspoon, for example). An infected cavity has less localized pain when tapped.

To soothe the pain, clean the tooth thoroughly (this will hurt) and **rinse with warm water, salt and a dissolved painkiller** such as acetaminophen. If the pain persists, **put a tablet of acetaminophen on the site of the infection and hold it in place with your tongue,** although oil of cloves is better if you have it.

You need dental treatment, either way. If the nearest dentist is three days away or more, you could consider inserting a temporary cement filling, as this will stop the infection spreading. This assumes you have a pack of IRM (a zinc oxide powder called "intermediate restorative material" by dentists) in your medical kit (and you should). **Remove as much decay as possible from the infected cavity** with a cotton swab drenched in alcohol. Again, this will hurt. Limited pain relief may be achieved by filling the cavity with a powdered painkilling pill. **Fill the cavity with IRM and tamp down as hard as you can** with a cotton ball or something similar.

If the toothache is severe enough to wake a sleeping sufferer, the tooth must come out. Use a pair of pliers and remember that it is like taking out a stubborn fence post: **wiggling it from side to side while exerting a smooth but strong upward (or downward for top teeth) pressure** will eventually loosen the tooth. It will come out with something of a crack. Stem the blood with cotton soaked in warm salty water.

... high fever

REALITY CHECK

A Red Cross delegate in one of the Rwandan refugee camps in Ngara, Western Tanzania, woke one morning with what he assumed was the flu and struggled in to work. He returned home at lunchtime and went to bed sweating. His fever deepened through the night and throughout the next day. According to colleagues who were checking up on him from time to time, he spent a second night shivering and feverish. The next morning, he was unconscious. And by lunchtime, he was dead. This was no flu; this was malaria, the particularly vicious kind called "cerebral" or *falciparum* malaria. This is no urban myth. It happens.

If you go down with a sudden-onset, shivering "fever of unknown origin" while working in an area endemic for malaria, you should assume malaria and seek medical attention. The (syndromic) **diagnosis must be that you have malaria *falciparum* and (presumptive) treatment should be prescribed accordingly**. Many people self-diagnose at this stage, but this is not to be encouraged.

Ideally, a **rapid blood test should be done**—larger refugee camps will have a basic laboratory where this and a blood-smear microscopic analysis can be done (though beware of false negative readings, which can be over 10 percent in such facilities)—before taking chemoprophylaxis, i.e., **swallowing a large dose (2,000 mg.) of Malarone** or something similar. (ACT, artemisenin combination therapies, are now used in quinine-resistant endemic areas.) **This first dose should be followed by 500 mg. every four hours for the next three days.** This dosage might make the patient dizzy for some days afterward and may cause liver damage if taken in excess.

Some of the most common vector-borne diseases are malaria, dengue, Japanese encephalitis and yellow fever. The vector is the mosquito. Female (not male) *Anopheles* mosquitoes transmit a single-celled parasite called *Plasmodium* (most commonly *vivax* or *falciparum*) that multiply in red blood cells, causing malaria. When a female mosquito sucks blood from an infected person, the malaria parasites reproduce in her body and find their way to the salivary glands. The next person to be bitten will therefore be injected with saliva carrying the parasite. (Some people think that HIV can be transmitted the same way. This is not true. If it were, the prevalence of HIV-AIDS would be much higher than it is.)The mosquitoes feed in the evenings and the mornings, unlike the *Aedes aegypti* mosquito (easily spotted by virtue of its black-and-white-striped rear legs), which feeds during the day and transmits the dengue virus. To give you malaria, the biting female (not the male, which drinks sap from plants), age between ten and twenty-seven days, must have had a blood-meal from a host (normally another human, a monkey or a cow) already infected with the *Plasmodium* parasite in the adult stage of its life cycle up to seventy-two hours earlier. The chances of all these conditions

being met is estimated to be 100:1 or more. In other words, on average, and even though one bite is enough to transmit the parasite, **only one bite in every hundred has the potential to infect**.

It is sobering to recall that the biggest killer disease in Sweden—a relatively cold Scandinavian country—two hundred years ago was malaria. Global climate change seems to be favoring the return of the mosquito to these northern latitudes. If this is true, then malaria will not be far behind. The best prophylaxis is to avoid being bitten in the first place. Most aid workers do not take chemoprophylaxis for any length of time if they live in endemic areas, preferring to **use roll-on DEET-based repellents, long pants and long sleeves in the evenings**. They also **sleep under insecticide-treated bed nets**, which are tied up during the day.

> **Aid professionals tend to cover up and use mosquito-repellent rather than take anti-malarials.**

Naturopaths prefer not to use powerful chemicals such as DEET. (I can understand why. When I used a 100 percent concentrate in Burundi, the plastic strap on my watch melted into my skin and I couldn't remove it for days!) Instead, they eat raw garlic and take Vitamin-B complexes such as Vegemite or Marmite; apparently, mosquitoes don't like the "yeasty" smell.

Bites are soothed with lavender oil and the juices of some fruits such as lemon and pawpaw, though an antihistamine cream is better. Meat tenderizer apparently works too (and is especially good for jellyfish stings), as the active ingredient, the enzyme papain, penetrates the skin to destroy the injected foreign protein that causes the bite's reaction.

Mosquitoes don't like smoke or, according to Papua New Guineans, tobacco. Perhaps this explains why so many aid workers smoke cigarettes. The Scots builders mending my mother's roof swear that a commercially available hand moisturizer containing isopropyl palmitate works just as well—at least against Scottish "midgies"—without any of the toxicity.

... crush injuries

Severe crush injuries cause extensive damage to skin, muscle, nerves and bone. There may be internal and external bleeding or blood supply to a limb may be cut off for some time. Large quantities of plasma may leak from the blood vessels into the damaged tissues, causing swelling and shock. When the crushed part is released, toxic chemicals produced by damaged muscles get into general circulation, and can cause kidney failure in severe cases.

If the crushed part has been trapped for more than thirty minutes, do not attempt to release the patient before medical help arrives. If there is no option but to release the patient immediately—as with earthquake victims, for example—**raise the affected limb** but **keep the victim still.** Try to **prevent bleeding** and **give as much comfort and reassurance as you can.**

... sexual assault

REALITY CHECK

This recent story was recounted by a trauma counselor, using a fictitious name to preserve doctor-patient confidentiality.

"Genevieve" was working for a French NGO in Liberia. She had been helping a traditional birth attendant deliver a child and was returning to base camp alone and rather later in the day than she should have been. The road had turned to mud, as it had rained that afternoon, and she got stuck. After she had called for help over the radio, she was abducted by two men at gunpoint in the dark while waiting to be rescued. She fought them but was overpowered. For three days, she was tied up in a hut without food or water and repeatedly raped. All she remembers from this ordeal is that she told herself over and over again that she "would not die" and that she "would not cry." On the fourth day, without warning, she was thrown in the back of a car and dumped, dazed and disoriented, with all her belongings, back at the same spot where she had been abducted. She was quickly found by her colleagues, who had been out looking for her all that time.

After medical checks and police statements had been made, she started on a course of "post-exposure prophylaxis" in case she had been infected with HIV. Her husband back in France begged her over the satellite phone to come home, but she refused, thinking that all she needed was a little time, and she had convinced herself that "the people needed her." After a few days of talking and talking to a couple of her female colleagues about what little she could remember of the ordeal, she decided to go back to work.

It immediately became obvious to her colleagues that she was confused, could not concentrate on what she was doing and was having difficulty remembering even the simplest instruction. At this point, she was medically evacuated.

Once home, her employer arranged for her to have professional counseling. Apparently, random sounds, sights and smells were triggering flashbacks that left her sobbing uncontrollably. According to her husband, she would wake screaming in the night. With me, she talked mostly about her guilt and stupidity for being out in the dark alone that night. She could not tell me what had happened to her because she could remember only pain and fear. She was suffering a severe form of post-traumatic stress disorder (PTSD).

With the help of her understanding husband and four months of therapy, she eventually appeared to recover and has even gone back to work in the agency's headquarters. But, as she says herself, "Nothing will be the same again."

Rape is an ugly, brutal and life-changing act of violence that involves sex. It is not a crime of passion but an expression of rage, hostility and power. Therefore it can happen to anyone at any time, without regard to age, appearance or behavior of the victim. Attempted rape is almost always a premeditated event, with over half of all attacks coming from someone known to the "target."

But, although there was little room for maneuver in the "reality check" above, certain actions can be taken to reduce the consequences of an attempted sexual assault:

> If someone is following behind you on a street or in a parking lot, or is with you in an elevator or stairwell, look him in the face and make small talk; perhaps ask him a question like "What time is it?" Once you've seen his face and could identify him in a lineup, you lose appeal as a target.

> If someone is coming toward you, hold out your hands in front of you and yell "stop" or "stay back" at the top of your voice. Most rapists said they would leave someone alone if they yelled or showed that they would not be afraid to fight back. They are looking for an easy target.

> If someone grabs you around the waist from behind, pinch the attacker either under the arm (between the elbow and armpit) or in the upper inner thigh as hard as you can. It hurts enough to cause him to let go.

> After the initial affront, go for the groin and kick the attacker's genitals as hard as you can. You might think that you'll make him angry and want to hurt you more, but it turns out that rapists are looking for someone who will not cause a lot of trouble. Start causing trouble and he's out of there.

> Alternatively, when the attacker's intentions are clear, appear to succumb—and even welcome—the advance. Let him put his hands up to your face, then grab his first two fingers and bend them back as far as you can. You are trying to break them, so use as much force as you possibly can. Try it out on a friend and see how quickly it works!

Most "foreign" rapists think international women are a "soft touch" and don't expect resistance. But if you scream and run, more often than not, so will they. The more effective the preventative measures and commonsense precautions you take, the lower your chance of becoming a victim.

Following sexual assault, it is natural to experience feelings of fear, pain, anger, shame and confusion. In addition, you will probably be asking yourself such questions as:

> Have I been exposed to a sexually transmitted disease?

> Could I have contracted the HIV virus?

> And if you are a woman, what are the chances of becoming pregnant?

All these concerns are legitimate and you will need a physician to assist you in addressing them.

Pregnancy is always a risk in women of childbearing age.

Fortunately, this risk can be eliminated by taking the so-called morning-after pill.

Becoming infected with a sexually transmitted disease is also a possibility. Fortunately, these diseases are easy to diagnose and to treat.

The exact risk of HIV infection following a sexual assault is not known, but it is estimated to be low—probably in the range of less than 1 percent. However, the chance of being exposed to the HIV virus increases if you:

> were assaulted by more than one man
> have damaged skin
> were anally assaulted
> suspect that the person who assaulted you is HIV positive or an injecting drug user

If the HIV status of the assailant is not known, HIV positivity must be assumed. If you were exposed to the virus, it may be possible to reduce the chances of getting the disease by taking anti-HIV medication. This post-exposure prevention (PEP) regimen is to be started within two to seventy-two hours after exposure and must continue for four weeks. Because of the potential side effects of these medications, evacuation to a place with better medical facilities may be necessary, since the followup involves laboratory testing and good administering practice. PEP treatment is an emergency medical response for individuals exposed to HIV and consists of medication, laboratory tests and counseling.

... **trauma and stress**

Those who deal with traumatic events such as pulling dead and/or decomposing bodies from the rubble of an earthquake or out of a water pond into which drowned bodies have been swept after a cyclone have a higher likelihood of developing psychological problems. I walked into my cousin's house recently and was hit by an overpowering smell of decomposition. The house had been empty for some weeks. At some point, an electrical surge had turned off the power to the freezer and rotting food was now leaking all over the floor. But the smell was exactly as I remembered from right after the earthquake in Pakistan, where thousands of people remained buried under the rubble and were decomposing in 100°F heat. I was immediately overwhelmed by the same feeling of helplessness that I experienced then and was unable to concentrate on my work for some days afterward.

A friend had been in the same town earlier than me, trying to dig people out from under the rubble. What she remembers is not the smell but the faint sounds of trapped people growing quieter and quieter. She has nightmares about this even now, five years after the event.

Doctors say those facing extremes of stress often change their behavior in an effort to find a new internal equilibrium. People feel shocked and numb, fearful and anxious, sometimes helpless and hopeless. They feel guilty. Sometimes they feel angry. As well as emotional reactions, there are psychological reactions to look out for, like poor concentration or poor memory. Some lose confidence. Others feel they have to be overvigilant. Generally, people suffering from extreme stress either regress into less mature patterns of behavior or begin to isolate themselves.

If such feelings persist, we should respect ourselves and those around us enough to **seek some form of professional counsel**.

Being involved in or witnessing incidents that involve direct threats to life or possible harm to you or others creates feelings of fear, horror, rage and powerlessness that have the potential to produce long-lasting and very serious emotional and/or psychological effects. When an incident has happened to you:

> Get away from the immediate scene of the incident. Allow yourself at least brief rest and respite. Use relaxation techniques to reduce anxiety (see page 82).

> Psychological reactions to traumatic incidents vary enormously. Understand that intense reactions (or even lack of immediate reaction) are normal, not a sign of weakness or of there being something wrong with you.

> Talk about what happened when you are ready, with someone who is willing to listen empathetically.

> Participate in crisis-intervention programs provided by your agency.

> Plan to return to work promptly, if at all possible.

> If you still are experiencing major distress after several weeks, seek professional help.

Research into the aftermath of the Kosovo War in 1999 suggests two groups of relief workers are most at risk of developing stress-related problems:

1. First-time volunteers, who may be wholly unprepared for the job, who do not know what to expect or who have unrealistic expectations of their own resilience.

2. More experienced experts from overseas who travel from disaster to disaster, and who as a result have probably built up cumulative amounts of stress without realizing it.

Cumulative stress can creep up on you and lead to "burnout." Such stressors can be:

> separation from family
> physically demanding working and living conditions
> lack of privacy and personal space
> long hours, heavy workloads, chronic fatigue
> lack of time, resources, support to do job
> conflict with supervisor or within work team
> conflicts with local authorities

> exposure to danger

> repeated exposure to tales of horrific experiences

> direct exposure to gruesome scenes and terrifying experiences

> moral anguish over choices made, and realization that you can't do it all

Techniques for preventing stressors from occurring, reducing the impact of stressors and coping better are the best protection. Solid social support and adequate rest and breaks from work are especially important. Monitor yourself for signs of burnout, "compassion fatigue" and secondary traumatization. These are signals that you need to change something—what you are doing or how you are doing it. Having recognized stress:

> take some time off—two days at least, and turn off your cell phone unless you want to talk to somebody

> get enough sleep and rest

> engage in "general" relaxation activities (games, sports, hobbies, socializing, music, journal writing, art)

> engage in vigorous exercise

> talk about your feelings

> pursue your spiritual interests and activities

> engage in relaxation exercises on a regular (daily) basis

> reduce your caffeine and/or nicotine intake

To help evaluate whether you or one of your colleagues are suffering from stress, sit down and talk through the following questions, giving a score of 1–4 (1 = never, 2 = once a month, 3 = once a week, 4 = all the time).

Symptom	Score
I feel tense and nervous	
I have physical aches and pains	
I always seem to be tired	

The smallest noise makes me jump

I am no longer interested in my work

I am beginning to be impulsive and don't care so much about risk

I can't get distressing events out of my mind

I get angry with myself for wanting to cry

I feel I am less efficient in my work. Small things seem to get on top of me, and even doing routine things is becoming an effort

I have trouble thinking clearly and cannot verbalize what I mean

I am having difficulty sleeping and am having bad dreams

I am cynical and overly critical about what my friends are doing

Minor inconveniences such as being stuck in traffic make me want to "explode"

I am spending more time at work

A stress-counseling session has been arranged, but I don't see the need to go (if yes, score 4)

Total score

If your aggregate score is:

less than 24 = this is normal given your working environment;

between 25 and 35 = you should discuss taking a break with your direct supervisor;

above 35 = you are under severe stress and may need medication. See a doctor.

Slowing down your respiratory rhythm slows your heart rate, and slows you down mentally and physically. The following routine reduces anxiety and can be used at any time, including just before public speaking:

> Put your feet flat on the floor, wiggle your toes one by one (which is almost physically impossible) and consciously relax your muscle groups—especially shoulder and buttock muscles—one by one. First back, then chest, belly, buttocks, legs and feet.

> Breathe in slowly and invisibly until your lungs are quite filled. Hold your breath for a count of five. Flex your fingers.

> Then breathe out slowly, as if through a straw, while counting down from five to one. Expel all the air from your lungs. Pause. And then repeat the exercise ten times. If public speaking, halfway through the exercise, focus on your first sentence and three things you want to say, and repeat them inwardly to yourself as a kind of mantra. It's amazing how, when your mind goes momentarily blank, these three things come back into your mind.

Stress reactions typically occur in five phases.

Pre-event: of varied duration, depending on how dangerous the environment is. There is a natural tendency to deny that anything could happen to oneself.

Warning: signs are increasing that something bad is going to happen. An atmosphere of panic begins to creep in.

Acute: this is the time that the person is exposed to the event. It could last seconds or days. People react differently to the physiological and mental shocks involved: 25 percent remain calm and continue to help others; 60 percent think they are calm but become apathetic and confused; 12 percent show such strong reactions that they need medical help; while 3 percent lose control and show signs of serious mental disturbance.

Interim: people start to reflect and realize what the event means to them. The initial reaction can last for up to six weeks, with the healing period taking many months.

Post-trauma: starts after about six months and can last indefinitely, although its occurrence depends in part on the effectiveness of the healing phase and the support given by family and friends. Symptoms of post-traumatic stress disorder include reliving the event, overreaction to sounds or smells, nightmares, a lack of interest in important events or others' lives, insomnia, verbal expressions of guilt, loss of memory and problems with concentration.

When it comes to trying to reduce the stress on field staff "in the front line," there are "commonsense" responses in which organizations or groups of coworkers can engage. These include making telecommunications equipment available so it is easier to call home, setting up peer-to-peer networks so people can discuss with others what they have been through, teaching stress-management techniques and creating a culture where people can talk about their feelings more readily.

If you are going home to recuperate from the aftereffects of a "critical incident," it is suggested that you read the **coming home** section at the end of this chapter. A less serious stress-busting self-help kit can be found at the back of the book.

... **nosebleeds**

Nosebleeds are triggered by any number of factors, principal among which is a combination of a rise in blood pressure (stress) and a dry atmosphere. Such conditions exist at high altitude or when exposure to air-conditioning has been prolonged.

The "pinching method" is the only generally accepted medical practice for stopping nosebleeds. It is not recommended that you tilt your head back while suffering a nosebleed (contrary to popular belief). This allows blood to flow into the esophagus and poses a choking hazard, as well as causing blood to collect in the stomach. Too much swallowed blood will cause vomiting. Tilt forward instead.

Block the blood flow with a small twist of toilet paper, cotton wool or something similar. Pinch your nose just below the bridge. There is a vein just below the nose bone that is the source of many bloody noses. Pinching puts pressure on it, which arrests the bleeding and speeds the clotting process. Do this for ten minutes. Try not to let go to see if the bleeding has stopped—it might start again. If the bleeding continues, pinch again for another ten minutes. If your nose is still bleeding, pinch for a further ten minutes. If the bleeding persists after half an hour, seek medical attention. If you can, hold some ice on the bridge of your nose (the bony part), as this constricts the blood vessels thereby reducing blood flow to the nostrils.

Once the flow has slowed, loosen the small nasal "rag" (but don't remove it completely), close your mouth and begin breathing slowly and deeply through your nose.

If all else has failed, you can try inhaling four shots of a decongestant spray while you think about seeking medical attention. Decongestant sprays contain oxymetazoline, which constricts blood vessels and stops bleeding within seconds. It is not recommended to use such sprays for longer than three to five days.

I've found that blowing my nose during a heavy nosebleed, dislodging built-up mucus, can make the bleeding stop much sooner than otherwise.

Once the flow has stopped and you have cleaned up, gently moisturize the inside of the affected nostril by applying a small amount of petroleum jelly. This moistens the nasal passages and minimizes the chance of the nosebleed recurring. Use your fingertip.

For a while afterward, avoid food or pills that raise the blood pressure temporarily (e.g., chocolate, coffee, ibuprofen).

... **alcohol**

This is not to suggest that what one does during the day is merely an interruption to taking on more alcohol, but a sober reflection on the consequences of reality. As stories elsewhere in this book point out, in some countries—particularly in the Caucasus and Central Asia— drinking can be an integral part of working, as well as social, life.

Not to "lose face" during an "access negotiation" in a conflict zone such as Chechnya, for example, sometimes requires drinking 45-proof alcohol at eight o'clock in the morning—especially during the winter.

Of course, avoiding alcohol in such cases would be the best course of action. But this is not always possible. In male-oriented societies, it is easier for women to decline—citing some "monthly" or medical problem—without jeopardizing the outcome of the meeting. For men to decline alcohol, even using some spurious medical excuse, is to challenge the hospitality of the host, and is therefore frowned upon.

Recognizing this, the only course of action is to mitigate or delay the effects of inevitable inebriation. The most effective way to do this is to **eat a bowl of what the Albanians call *kos* and the Georgians call *mastoni* (a mixture of curds and yogurt) prior to taking on alcohol**—but don't let anyone see you do it as it's considered unmanly.

Somewhere in the cheese-making process there is an interim stage during which milk separates to form a jellyish slime of curd and an opaque liquid called whey. This slime is the fundamental ingredient of *kos*. You can make it yourself by adding a large spoonful of active curd to a bowl of just boiled full-fat milk and leaving it in a warm room overnight (but using unpasteurized milk in areas where brucellosis is endemic is not advised). Alternatively, you can eat a cup of yogurt from a shop, but this is not as effective. Less effective still is the milk itself, but even this is better than nothing. Italians often take a shot of neat olive oil instead. The higher the fat content of what you ingest, the longer you will stave off getting drunk. In fact, you might avoid it altogether.

There are alternatives, of course. You can always dump the alcohol in a nearby flowerpot, or

Eat a bowl of curds before drinking alcohol.

just sip rather than "down in one." But both these mitigation behaviors are likely to be noticed and you will be taken less seriously if they are.

In some West African countries, "toasts" are made with palm wine during important events. This involves pouring the first and last sip of the drink onto the ground to honor the ancestors. I have a friend who was soon known across the district for being "extremely generous to the ancestors"—face-saving rather than insulting.

If all else has failed and you wake up with a splitting headache, not knowing where you are or how you got there, you have a hangover. This is the result of dehydration. The cure, therefore, is to rehydrate as quickly as possible. And the best way to do this is to **drink one liter (two if you can manage it without throwing up) of dissolved oral rehydration salts (ORS)**. According to some in the international health community, the powder in this little "miracle packet" has saved the lives of more children than any other single medical intervention in the world—ever. More so even than antibiotics or mosquito bed nets. And it will "save" you.

The only thing more effective than drinking large quantities of ORS is to rehydrate using an intravenous drip on its maximum setting. Even with a doctor on your team, this is not likely to be available—although I did work with a young medic from the British NGO Merlin who once admitted to doing this while at medical school. Alternative measures include "topping up" with a shot of vodka or olive oil, eating fatty food such as egg, bacon and fries or drinking spicy tomato juice. In my experience, the ORS are best.

... **personal hygiene**

When the men with whom you share a guesthouse have used up all the toilet paper without telling anyone, use your hands and water instead. Next best is pre-scrunched squares of newspaper or money. Do not attempt to flush these, however. After that, use your imagination.

When that last precious tampon has been used, resort to ropes of twisted (clean) rag or make a sanitary pad from cotton wool wrapped in gauze, muslin or even toilet paper. Ripped-off shirtsleeves work quite well, I'm told.

When using a pit-latrine, the trick is to squat all the way down on your haunches so that your backside is touching your heels, which are flat on the "slab" (there will be a porcelain slab with footholds if you are lucky; wooden poles if you are not); do not, as so many Westerners do, balance on the balls of your feet with your backside half suspended. If you do this, your leg muscles will begin to shake before you're finished and you'll be keeping your balance with one hand on some unsavory brickwork in places you cannot see. Second, and much more important, you will miss—with unfortunate consequences. Some Westerners balance using flat stones under each heel that they then place to one side for use next time, or kick into the pit once finished. Some pit-latrines are "dry" and some "wet." If there is a bucket of water around, it is "wet," so wipe using your hand and flush using the dipper provided. Try to resist the temptation to wash your hands in the bucket. Again, use the dipper as this prevents the spread of water-borne diseases. Paper should not be flushed down a pit-latrine as it disrupts the natural composting cycle. Instead, place in a bucket for burning later. Same with tampons.

Regular washing of clothes, especially underwear, is crucial to the maintenance of personal hygiene. Ironing of underwear is especially important in some parts of the tropics as some nasty little "biting bugs" can survive among the stitching and these can only be killed by the application of heat. If, for some reason, this is not possible, the last resort is to do what mountaineers do and "invert and reverse." This involves turning underpants inside out every second day and reversing them every fourth day. Chaffing and natural decomposition will minimize risk of local skin infection if this is done.

Armies lose more soldiers to foot rot and sexually transmitted infections than bullet wounds. To prevent the former when working in extremely isolated places that are either cold or wet, sprinkle (dry) feet with liberal doses of fungicidal powder from time to time. Do this as a preventive measure, i.e., before any infection occurs. To prevent the latter, use a condom.

Condoms are also useful for keeping cell phones dry or storing water.

The result of poor personal hygiene practice is directly related to what WHO calls "onset of diarrheal disease" but what we call the "runs." Most such episodes result from eating fruit and vegetables or drinking water contaminated with "fecal coliforms," 99 percent of which are *E. coli*. **Drink and brush your teeth with bottled water**, therefore, having first checked that the seal is unbroken.

Eat only freshly cooked hot food and avoid unpeeled salads. When stopping for refreshment in some local shack, don't be embarrassed to wipe clean teaspoons and glasses before use as the water used for washing is doubtless contaminated. The biggest mistake of all is to mix a drink with locally manufactured ice. In India, my grandmother, bless her, used to take a gin and tonic every evening during the last days of the Raj at six o'clock sharp, with the ice secured inside a condom (presumably they weren't coated in lubricants and spermicides in those days?!).

... relaxing

After three weeks of 24/7 relief operations, it's okay to have a day off. In fact, the U.S. Office for Foreign Disaster Assistance (OFDA) in Washington has an unwritten rule that you must take one day off in every seven after the first three weeks of deployment. You are expected to turn your phone (and BlackBerry) off, not use a laptop (i.e., no emails), and to keep them off all day.

In the UN system, periods of R&R (rest and recuperation)

> **Take at least one day off every week after three weeks in the field.**

away from the zone of operations, set by the resident humanitarian coordinator, are considered essential to the sustainability of human resourcing in the field and are obligatory. Only a fool denies that these are necessary. Unfortunately, many do, insisting that their job is too important to leave. As the European Commission discovered when surveying stress during the Bosnian conflict, it is such people who burn out and end up jeopardizing both their long-term health and the relief operations they manage (see **trauma and stress** section).

It is always a good idea to carry a pack of playing cards; someone will know how to play twenty-one or Texas hold'em (a form of poker). Other two-player favorites are chess, Connect Four and backgammon. One of the simplest and most relaxing multiple-player games—especially when working in multicultural settings—is Rummikub®, which can also be played with two sets of playing cards. All are available in miniature versions.

No aid worker appears to be without an iPod nowadays. A docking station with miniature speakers for broadcasting music is a welcome addition and makes you popular.

For those who like to "get away from it all" by going fishing, a collapsible fishing rod comes into its own. If this is too over the top, just use the hook and line from your survival kit.

... **sleeping**

To ensure a sound night's sleep, use a silk (not cotton) sleeping-bag liner and a cotton pillowcase. Silk has better thermal-retention properties than cotton, so a silk liner can be used in hot and cold climates. It also dries quicker than cotton and is lighter.

If there are mosquitoes around, sleep underneath a properly hung insecticide-treated bed net. Set up the net using drawing pins and dental floss. Dental floss is stronger and lighter than string or elastic cord (it is also better than cotton thread for sewing on buttons).

Pop in some foam earplugs and pull down those airline eyeshades to enjoy a good night's sleep—even in a dormitory of snoring men. A dab of lavender oil on the pillow works miracles when the feet of the person sleeping next to you are inches from your face—ask any of the earthquake responders who lived in the UN compound in Muzaffarabad, Pakistan.

If staying in cold climates, such as Central Asia during the winter, when nighttime temperatures frequently dip below 5°F(−15°C), it is not uncommon to find there is little in the way of heating in the room. Those used to such situations choose rooms on the floor above the kitchen or the reception as these areas are the warmest places in a hotel. Filling a couple of empty plastic bottles with hot water and using them as improvised hot-water bottles will help considerably in getting a good night's sleep.

... **coming home**

Coming home from a lengthy or particularly stressful mission abroad is a dislocating experience. Aid workers, stabilization advisers, soldiers and foreign correspondents witness some of the worst of humanity in some of the most remote and underprivileged regions of the world. They then "suffer" the surreal and distorting experience of rejoining the "normal" world of family and friends, who tend to have little interest in, and even less knowledge of, where they have been or what they have just been through.

If the mission was to a conflict zone, there is a tendency to be hypervigilant upon return. Unexpected noises make you flinch and you find yourself looking at people and things as if they are a threat. A car pulls up next to you at the traffic lights and you notice that the occupants are looking oddly at you. Then, in a flash of guilty recognition, you realize that it is you who has been looking oddly at them—unconsciously checking to see whether they have guns or not.

For some weeks, you will be prone to weird dreams. Not just prompted by the recent sight of dead bodies either, but often involving noises and smells experienced years before.

Adjusting to the dislocation of coming home requires compromise on both sides.

As a member of the returnee's family, you have faced your own challenges in keeping your family functioning while your loved one is away. Reunions following deployment are usually eagerly anticipated by all. However, they are sometimes more complicated than you may think. When welcoming a loved one who is returning from disaster-relief work, keep the following in mind. The points are valid for both parties:

> Homecoming is more than an event; it is a process of reconnection for family and loved ones.

> Though coming home represents a return to safety, security and "normality," the routines at home are markedly different from life in a disaster zone.

> In your loved one's absence, you and your family members have assumed many roles and functions that may now have to be renegotiated. Be patient during this period and recognize that many things do not return, at least immediately, to what they were previously.

> Go slowly. Your returning loved one, you and your family need time— time together if possible—before exposure to the demands of the larger community, friends, extended family and coworkers.

> Celebrating a homecoming is important and should reflect your own family's style, preferences and traditions.

> In the disaster environment, it is common to talk about things that may be upsetting to people not directly involved (e.g., dead bodies, graphic images). Extreme care should be taken by returning family members (monitored by their loved ones) to ensure that relating experiences does not unnecessarily upset or traumatize others. This is especially important in discussing the experience with or in the presence of children.

> Talking about disaster experiences is a personal and delicate subject. Many people prefer to share such experiences with a coworker or friend. Some may want to talk at length about their experience.

Sometimes the need/desire to talk about experiences will vacillate a great deal. Let your returning loved one take the lead. Listening rather than asking questions is the guiding rule.

> When talking about your experiences, keep it short. If the listener wants to know more, they will ask. Try not to be offended—as I was—by others' apparent inability to relate to your experience; however hard they try, they simply cannot visualize the psychological or physical place you have just returned from. The human brain also has limited capacity to process what your words are describing.

> It is wise to keep your social calendar fairly free and flexible for the first weeks after the homecoming. Respect the need for time alone and time with especially important people, such as spouses. Explain to those who may feel slighted that this is a normal requirement of returning personnel.

> Your returning loved one may need time to adjust to the local time zone, as well as environmental changes such as continuous noise or interruption.

> Your children's reactions may not be what you or the returning loved one may have expected or desired. Very often children will act shy at first. Older children may feel and act angry that their parent has been absent. Be patient and understanding concerning reactions and give everyone time to get reacquainted.

> Be flexible and keep expectations reasonable. It is normal to experience some disappointment or letdown when homecomings are not what you had hoped. The reality of homecoming and reunion seldom match one's fantasies and preconceived scenarios. This is particularly noticeable when you are home only for a few days—as when on R&R, for example.

Leaving home once again and returning to the site of a disaster or other location is stressful for everybody. It is natural to feel sad or angry, and partners are prone to fight and argue—both the one leaving and the one being left behind. You have drawn close once again and begun to establish routines. Your loved one may psychologically and/or emotionally distance himself/herself in preparation for leaving. Try to understand if this happens.

At the time of departure, it is important that you let your loved one know how proud you are of his/her sacrifice and commitment to the work. Expressing pride while saying good-bye is positive, and will give everyone strength during the coming separation.

Recognize when to seek help. Remember, pre- or post-deployment stress is a normal reaction to abnormal situations like disasters. But if you or a deployed family member experience the following signs of persistent or severe stress, seek help from a licensed mental-health professional:

> disorientation (e.g., dazedness, memory loss, inability to give date/ time or recall recent events)

> depression (e.g., pervasive feeling of hopelessness and despair, withdrawal from others)

> anxiety (e.g., being constantly on edge, feeling restless, obsessive fear of another disaster)

> acute psychiatric symptoms (e.g., hearing voices, seeing visions, delusional thinking)

> inability to care for oneself (e.g., not eating, bathing, changing clothing or handling other aspects of daily life)

> suicidal or homicidal thoughts or plans

> problematic use of alcohol or drugs

> domestic violence, child abuse or elder abuse

> sleeplessness and recurrent nightmares

When asked why you choose to live your life this way, there is no need to be defensive. Journalists, aid workers and others share a feeling that they are bearing witness to and/or making a genuine difference at the cutting edge of history—and, in their own way, they are. Idealism is a genuine motivation, too, with only the most cynical questioning this. It may be worth admitting, though, that you are just too antisocial to fit into normal society. . . .

How to deal with...

Contrary to popular belief, the frequency of natural disasters is *not* increasing around the world, but their ferocity is. Situated in an unstable volcanic zone and surrounded by large masses of deep and warm water, Southeast Asia bears the brunt of these events, although other areas of the world where tectonic plates collide are hardly immune to the effects of earthquakes. Perhaps these weather events are linked to global warming, perhaps not. Perhaps some events are man-made? I once overheard a visiting dignitary tell President Pervez Musharraf, the then-president of Pakistan, that the earthquake in Kashmir in 2005 was the direct consequence of underground nuclear testing assumed to be going on in the area.

Sea levels are rising, glaciers are melting and cyclones are becoming more powerful. This leaves low-lying countries like Bangladesh and Myanmar highly vulnerable, not just to the devastating effects of wind but also to tidal storm surges that push 10-foot-high walls of seawater farther inland than they ever went before. Construction of high-rise buildings in places like Tirana in Albania and Bishkek in Kyrgyzstan rarely conform to the standards of construction needed to make them seismic-resistant, with the result that they are bound to collapse if struck by even a medium-size earthquake.

... **earthquakes**

If you are indoors, stay there and **do not run outside,** where falling debris—especially roof tiles—can often inflict more harm than collapsing buildings. The possible exception is if you are in a one-story bungalow in a remote area. In this situation, it's a judgment call, but you should consider exiting if you physically can.

If you are in a high-rise building, **do not run downstairs or try to take the elevator. Move into a doorway or a corner of a room** as these are structurally the strongest places in a room.

Next best is to crawl under a stout table or desk or behind a high-backed sofa. At least this will provide partial protection from falling debris. Whichever you choose, hang on to it tight as it too will start bouncing across the floor.

If you are living in an earthquake-prone area such as Jakarta in Indonesia, **do not stay in a building between three and eight stories** in height. Shake-tests conducted by structural engineers indicate that these buildings are most at risk of collapse, while many taller buildings are better able to absorb the ground oscillations produced by earthquakes without catastrophic failure.

> **If you are in a high-rise building when an earthquake hits, do not take the elevator or run downstairs.**

If you are outside, get into the open, away from buildings, power lines, chimneys, trees and anything else that could fall on you. Be aware of the strong likelihood of aftershocks and be ready to run away from landslides. In the Pakistan earthquake of 2005, landslides claimed almost as many lives as collapsing buildings.

> **Falling roof tiles and tetanus can kill just as many people as collapsing buildings.**

When everything has become quiet, render what first aid you can. **Don't let people smoke**, because gas lines are likely to have been ruptured. Post-earthquake fire killed three times more people than collapsing buildings during the 1995 earthquake in Kobe, Japan.

When you can, make sure to **wear heavy shoes**, as puncture wounds from exposed nails, shards of glass and other sharp objects can cause tetanus. In fact, tetanus was the biggest cause of avoidable death after the Indonesian earthquake of 2006.

If water is readily available, **damp down debris**—in developing countries there will probably be asbestos in the dust from fallen buildings. And inhaled asbestos will kill you as surely as a falling roof tile, only more slowly.

When responding to the aftermath of an earthquake and having to live in the affected area, it is better to **live in a tent outside** than inhabit a structurally damaged house, which may collapse during the next aftershock. You can use what toilet and/or washing facilities remain functional in any nearby building. If you venture inside a damaged building, ensure there are no cracks wide enough to insert a clenched fist. If there are, don't go in.

If driving, especially in steep-sided mountainous areas, **pull over into the mountainside of the road. Stay in the car** as loose rocks will tumble down the mountainside for some time and the car affords some protection. If you are near a road tunnel, drive a short way into it, then stop, as falling rocks cannot reach you in there. It is highly unlikely to be blocked by rock fall, and if it is, the chances of the other end being blocked too are infinitesimal.

REALITY CHECK

I experienced my first earthquake while driving in Albania. At first I thought the car's suspension had broken. As I slowed to investigate, we came around a corner to find the concrete bridge in front of us swaying. The suspension was clearly not the problem.

At the same instant, large boulders started slamming into the road around us. Happily for me and my three passengers, we were able to park the car under a large rocky overhang and did not suffer a scratch. Years later, some weeks after the 2005 Pakistan earthquake, a friend of mine was in a car pulverized by a boulder loosened by an aftershock. He climbed out, but the driver was not so lucky.

... cyclones, hurricanes and typhoons

According to the Atlantic Oceanographic and Meteorological Laboratory, "hurricane" and "typhoon" are simply different names for a tropical cyclone. As a general rule, these cyclones are given the name "hurricane" in the western hemisphere (the North Atlantic Ocean, the Northeast Pacific Ocean east of the dateline or the South Pacific Ocean east of 160ºE) and the term "typhoon" is applied in the eastern hemisphere (the Northwest Pacific Ocean west of the dateline). Where wind speeds are lower than 75 miles per hour (33 meters per second), such cyclones are called "tropical depressions." At some point, increasing wind speeds turn a "depression" into a "storm," at which point they are given a local name according to a sequenced list maintained by the World Meteorological Organization. A "tropical cyclone" is the generic term for a nonfrontal synoptic-scale low-pressure system over tropical or subtropical waters with organized convection (i.e., thunderstorm activity) and definite cyclonic surface-wind circulation. There. Now you know.

If you are lucky enough to be in a solid brick or concrete-built structure, **stay indoors**, as the principal threat is from flying debris, especially corrugated-iron sheeting, which can cut people in half when whirling through the air. **Open windows a few inches.** This allows for quicker pressure equalization, which reduces the chance of the building literally imploding.

If caught outdoors, **tie yourself to a tree** or other fixed object with a rope or cable in the lee of the wind. If forced to use your belt, take it off, loop it around the fixed object and wrap the rest around one wrist. Hold on with both hands when you are about to be blown off your feet.

Alternatively, get as low as you can and wedge yourself in a ditch or in the lee of a large rock. Lie facedown with your hands clasped behind your head.

... volcanic eruption

REALITY CHECK

Goma in Eastern Congo (DRC), scene of the world's largest refugee outflows during the Rwanda genocide, was cut in half by a 10-foot-high wall of lava in 2003. Weeks later, the blackened basalt was still too hot to walk on. My favorite bar lies under that basalt.

Helping the people of Yogyakarta recover from the earthquake of May 2006, I stayed in one of the only undamaged hotels available. I could see the smoldering crater and occasional burps of lava from Mount Merapi from my bedroom window.

Molten rock (lava) flows like a viscous liquid: the hotter it is, the faster it flows. Eruption temperature is in the region of 2,100°F (1,150°C) and its rate of cooling will depend on the course it takes on its inevitable journey to the sea. In the open, lava will flow at about 6 miles per hour. If it is following a channel, it can reach 35 miles per hour. An athlete runs the 4-minute mile at about 16 miles per hour and the 100-meter world champion runs at 26 miles per hour. Work it out. Usually it is possible to jog—or even walk briskly—out of the way. But which way?

Like any liquid, lava will follow the path of least resistance and will therefore follow riverbeds and larger irrigation ditches. Locals living on the fertile slopes of active volcanoes (and they do, not necessarily because they are poor but because volcanic ash is a great natural fertilizer) know this and evacuate at the last possible moment, **not down but to one side**.

A pyroclastic eruption, however, is an entirely different affair. Such an eruption sees an explosive high-speed avalanche of hot ash, rock fragments and gas rolling down the sides of a mountain at speeds of over 150 miles per hour. Nothing in the path of such a "cloud," where temperatures exceed 1,800°F (980°C), survives. If a volcano has been declared unstable and has a history of pyroclastic eruption, do not venture closer than 3 miles (5 kilometers) from its base at any time.

Disaster

... **tsunami**

The first sign of an impending tsunami is often a seemingly innocuous receding of the sea. Depending on the slope of the seashore, the water may recede to the horizon. If you see either this or a large wave coming toward you, **run and scramble to the highest point** you can reach, **shouting a warning to others** as you do so. Aim for solid ground (a hill), a concrete building or a tree, in that order of priority. Although tsunamis travel through the open ocean at up to 650 miles per hour, the "wave" slows as it reaches shore to around 30 miles per hour. More than 100,000 tons of seawater bearing down on you at even this relatively slow speed is enough to obliterate all but the most solidly constructed buildings. Stay put—the initial wave will not only not recede but may also be followed by three or four more of equal or greater severity at intervals of up to twenty minutes. These waves may also "rebound" and come back again from the opposite direction.

> **A tsunami is not a wave. It looks like a wave at first, but you quickly realize that there is a solid wall of water behind it. And it just keeps coming.**
> (tsunami survivor, Sri Lanka)

101

... avalanches

Avalanches occur most often in areas of new snowfall, on north-facing slopes (70 percent occur here), in the leeward side (the side sheltered from the wind) of steep mountains, where the slope is greater than 35 degrees, and on the afternoons of sunny days on east-facing slopes, when the morning's sunlight may have loosened the "slip boundaries" between the different snow layers that have accumulated with successive snowfalls. Such accumulations can be highly unstable.

If you are caught in an avalanche, **"swim" freestyle as hard as you can to stay on top of the tumbling snow**. The snow can move at speeds of up to 95 miles per hour and acts like water when it is moving but solidifies once it stops as the crystals change shape.

As it begins to slow and stop—according to the Canadian lady quoted in the "reality check" above, you can tell by the reduction in noise from deafening to crackling silence—hold your arms in front of your face and try to create an air-filled space around your mouth. Then, if you can, create an air hole to the surface. Spit to work out which way is up.

If you can dig, do so. And do it quickly. In most cases, survival depends on someone else digging you out. Even without an air pocket, there is enough oxygen dissolved in the snow to maintain life for 45 minutes or more. In statistical terms, the victim has a 90 percent chance of survival if rescued within 15 minutes, which drops to less than 30 percent after 45 minutes. For those doing the searching, this means don't stop probing and don't stop searching.

Never venture into zones of high avalanche risk alone and/ or without the right equipment. And avoid obvious snow chutes where there are signs of recent slippage or rock fall. Stay below the treeline if possible. A "chunk" of snow the size of an armchair can weigh 1 ton or more. The momentum of such a block traveling at such speed will snap a fully grown pine tree as if it were a matchstick. Hiding behind trees therefore affords next to no protection.

> There is enough oxygen dissolved in snow to maintain life for up to 45 minutes.

If you are forced to stay overnight in the mountains, find shelter— preferably below the treeline—and stay warm and dry. Snow will only get deeper as you climb higher. The key to survival is keeping your head warm and staying out of the wind. If it is snowy, don't try to build a snow cave as this will cause you to sweat and the sweat will then freeze. Instead, **dig a shallow trench. Pile the snow upwind and uphill. Insulate the floor, get in and cover yourself.** Branches and leaves work well. Stay out of valleys and gullies as, with cold air collecting in low-lying areas, these are the coldest parts of the mountain. Do not be shy about sharing bodily warmth. If you are not alone, huddle together (see **hypothermia** section).

... biological, chemical and radiological attack

The chemical ricin has been used as a terror weapon in Japan. Biological weapons such as anthrax have killed people and caused chaos in the U.S. So far, no terror group has attached radioactive material to a conventional bomb—making a so-called dirty bomb— but it is possible.

Chemical agents are natural or manufactured chemicals that can be released in liquid, powder or aerosol form. Biological agents are naturally occurring germs, such as smallpox, which cause rare diseases with high death rates. Neither is easy to store or release, and although some, like anthrax, are more "persistent" than others, most degrade quickly when exposed to air and sunlight.

Move at least half a mile crosswind from the suspected blast or release site. Move to high ground.

Chemical attacks can cause breathing difficulties, eye and skin irritation, blisters, headaches, nausea and convulsions. The time it takes for symptoms to develop depends on the chemical and on its concentration, but unlike biological agents, chemical agents are not infectious. The symptoms of biological agents vary with each disease and are the same as when the disease is caught naturally. Antibiotics can be used to treat most biological-agent diseases. The sooner they are taken, the more effective they will be.

Antibiotics can be used to treat most biological-agent diseases. The sooner they are taken, the more effective they will be.

Aid agencies had to plan and train for decontamination scenarios during the last Iraq War, and the delayed threat to health posed by exposure to spent depleted-uranium ammunition in Kosovo and yellowcake in Baghdad has yet to be evaluated.

There is no guaranteed way of surviving a biological, chemical or radiological attack. All you can do is try to minimize the risk by **getting**

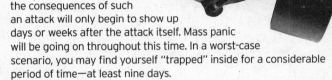

out of the affected area or sealing yourself indoors. Anywhere upwind will do in the case of chemical and biological agents, as these are most likely to be airborne. In the case of a dirty bomb, put at least 2 miles between you and the blast site. But much will depend on wind speed and direction. In most cases, the consequences of such an attack will only begin to show up days or weeks after the attack itself. Mass panic will be going on throughout this time. In a worst-case scenario, you may find yourself "trapped" inside for a considerable period of time—at least nine days.

Disaster

The basic rules to surviving are the same for each type of threat:

> **If you are outside, immediately enter a house or building.** Take a VHF handheld radio with you.

> If there's no safe building nearby, try to determine the direction of the wind, **get into a vehicle, close windows, vents and air-conditioning and move crosswind**, as this gives the greatest chance of getting out of the contaminated cloud quickly.

> **Avoid low-lying areas**, as the gases are usually heavier than air and may become trapped there. Upstairs is therefore better than downstairs.

> When inside a building, shut and lock all doors and windows. Turn off air conditioners, heaters, ventilation systems, all electrical appliances and close all water and gas taps. **Seal ventilators with tape and preferably do the same around the doors and windows.** If possible, **place damp towels at the bottom of doors**.

> If you have to go outside, breathing through a doubled-up and wetted T-shirt will greatly increase your chances of survival. However, this method isn't effective against most chemical agents.

> Cooperate with official instructions and stay put until you're given the all-clear by an official authority. Be prepared to evacuate if given

105

the official order to do so, but you will have to be decontaminated as a precaution before being allowed outside any quarantine zone.

> Minimize contact with other people and, once sealed indoors, don't let anyone else in.

> Maintain simple hygiene practices such as hand washing, as these decrease your chances of infection.

> Tune in to a local radio station that is broadcasting official emergency information.

> If you've been contaminated with hazardous materials, you'll greatly improve your chances of survival by conducting personal decontamination. In most cases, taking off your clothes and burning them will remove 80–90 percent of the potential contamination. Then wash yourself with water (or soap and water if possible).

... **wildfires**

Don't underestimate the speed with which a small brush fire can become an out-of-control inferno. Ask anybody who was unlucky enough to be in California or Greece in the summer of 2008. Fire can easily move faster than you, and embers can "jump" to cause fire to break out behind you. Fire fronts change rapidly depending on the wind and local topography.

If you see smoke, smell smoke or hear fire, **leave the area immediately** by the lowest route possible. But **avoid narrow valleys and steep slopes** as these areas act like a chimney for fires.

If in a car, **tightly close all windows and vents into the car**. If you have time, **remove any synthetic fibers that are next to your skin and wrap yourself in a dry blanket. Lie down on the floor.** Don't panic. As the fire passes over/around your car, the winds will rock it wildly. After the fire passes, get out of and away from the (now burning and very hot) car in case the fuel ignites.

Alternatively, look for a sizable body of water (a puddle won't help much as it will boil) or a depressed area and lie down. If there are neither nearby, clear an area between 10 and 20 feet around you of all burnable materials and lie facedown. Try to cover yourself with dirt. If you are caught and must go to ground within a 10 to 20-foot cleared space, remember that the fire will suck oxygen out of this area for a few minutes. Don't panic—oxygen will rush in as the fire passes.

As when working in any remote area, always let someone know where you are and keep your cell phone, handheld VHF radio and GPS fully charged.

If you or someone near you is on fire, remember:

> **Stop.** Don't panic and don't run about, as this fans the flames.
> **Drop.** Fall quickly to the ground or floor. If someone else is on fire, try to get them to do so. "Tackle" them only if you will not catch fire yourself.
> **Roll.** Roll (back and forth) until the fire is extinguished. The rolling will smother and scatter the fire in most cases. Use water, sand or a blanket to help smother the fire while others are rolling. Do not attempt to beat the fire out with bare hands; continue rolling instead.

If you catch fire, stop, drop and roll. Smother flames with a blanket.

... **electrical storms**

REALITY CHECK

In the North-West Frontier Province of Pakistan in July 2007, 250 villagers were avoiding flash floods during the monsoon when they were caught in an electrical storm. More than eighty of them died after they, and the corrugated-iron-roofed houses they were sheltering in, were hit by lightning.

More people are killed each year from lightning strikes than from hurricanes. And, contrary to popular belief, lightning does strike in the same place twice if that place is high and exposed.

Lightning heats the air around it to temperatures five times hotter than the sun. This heat causes the surrounding air to rapidly expand and vibrate, which creates thunder. Each bolt of lightning contains up to one billion volts of electricity. This enormous electrical discharge is caused by an imbalance between positive and negative charges. During a storm, colliding particles of rain, ice or snow in a cloud build up static electricity and increase this imbalance, with a negative charge collecting toward the base of the cloud. At the same time, objects on the ground become positively charged—creating an imbalance (a potential difference) that nature seeks to remedy by passing current between the two.

Nowhere is completely safe from lightning, although a building with a metal lightning conductor fitted to the exterior is safest. When the flashes are almost continuous, or the crash of thunder comes at the same time as the flash—sound travels at approximately 375 yards (340 meters) per second—you should have already sought shelter.

Avoid water and high or open places. If you are caught in the open, don't lie flat but squat on the balls of your feet, keeping your head down and your elbows in—this minimizes the chance of your body becoming a lightning conductor. If wearing insulated boots, so much the better. **Do not stand under trees**, especially lone trees.

> **If in the open during an electrical storm crouch down on the balls of your feet.**

Car tires afford excellent electrical insulation. **If you are near a vehicle and there is nowhere else to take shelter, inside it will probably be the safest place to be. Keep the windows rolled up and make sure you don't touch any metal surfaces.** If radio antennae are fitted, do not attempt to remove them at this stage (though you could have done this earlier as the storm approached).

Chapter 4

Personal Security

How to deal with...

Staying in the grandest hotels or the humblest guesthouses in many parts of Africa, Central America and South or Southeast Asia no longer isolates you from the politically or economically inspired motives of today's terrorists and criminals. Flying bullets and hand grenades are no longer confined to war zones, and even New Yorkers are expected to know how to react calmly to bomb threats. The sections that follow may help mitigate the worst effects of those risks you may potentially have to confront, whatever reason you may have for traveling through.

... **being shot at**

REALITY CHECK

I was first deliberately shot at as a military peacekeeper in Beirut in 1983. It is not a pleasant experience. The unmistakable and very loud *crack* above your head—much like the sound of a lion tamer's bullwhip in a circus—is the sound of a high-velocity (rifle) bullet just missing you. You will not hear the bullet that hits you, even if it is low-velocity (i.e., from a handgun), so don't hang around waiting to see if you can.

A German colleague and I were sniped at while trying to string a water pipe over the Neretva River, which divides the town of Mostar in Bosnia-Hercegovina, during the Yugoslav War in 1992. We were standing on the riverbank just above the famous Stari Most ("Old Bridge") when the shots came. Recognizing the sound, I shouted a warning to my startled colleague and ran for cover as fast as I could. Moments later, he—a man much larger and of more "generous proportions" than me—overtook me at some speed. I remember the 20 pounds of protective armor bouncing on his Bavarian beer belly as if it were nothing more cumbersome than a loose-fitting T-shirt. Fear is a remarkable motivator.

If you are indoors, and bullets or shrapnel are flying around, **find cover, get down and stay down**. It sounds obvious, but many people seem initially dazed and don't do so immediately. Some, like the foolish and overly macho ex-Foreign Legionnaire in Baghdad who took a bullet through the arm in front of me while watching Iraqis celebrate the capture of Saddam Hussein's sons by spraying bullets randomly in the streets, actually go outside to see what's going on. **If there is a bathtub nearby, preferably a metal (enameled) one, crawl over to it and get in**. You may have seen Bruce Willis doing this in one of the *Die Hard* movies. Turn on the tap to **fill it with water**; firefights can go on for over half an hour and water will afford additional protection. . . . There is a misshapen bullet on my desk that attests to the protective effectiveness of a bathtub!

As the story in the previous paragraph makes clear, "celebration" in some countries involves firing weapons of all makes and sizes indiscriminately into the air. Six people were killed in Zagreb, Croatia, on New Year's Eve in 1993 when out celebrating on the streets—as I was—by bullets falling back to earth. A bullet falling back to earth under no force but gravity still has enough kinetic energy to kill you if it hits you on your head. **If you are in a country where people insist on celebrating by firing guns in the air, make sure you—and your vehicle—are under cover when they do so.**

If someone deliberately points a gun at you, remember that most automatic weapons fire high and to the right after the first few rounds unless strongly controlled by the firer. This is because of the considerable clockwise "torque" effect imparted to the spinning bullet by the barrel's "rifling"—bullets are spun to increase their stability in flight.

For all their bravado, most gunmen are not sufficiently adept at controlling long bursts of automatic fire, with the result that the accumulating torque effect forces the barrel up and to the

If shot at, dive down to your right.

right. That is why experienced gunmen fire frequent short bursts rather than single long ones. **If there is some cover available, therefore, dive down and to your right (i.e., to the gunman's left) to shelter behind it.** If you are outdoors, getting between a car wheel and the gutter may be enough. But don't think for a moment that a car will protect you. Unlike in the movies, in real life high-velocity bullets pass straight through car doors.

If you have no other option, **run away in a straight line. When you have opened up a gap of at least 25 yards, start weaving** as you run. **Turn a corner as soon as you can**, taking yourself out of the line of sight. It is very difficult to take aim at a moving target that continually changes direction, especially when the range is farther than 25 yards.

If you are considered to be at high risk and have therefore been offered body armor (otherwise known as a bulletproof vest or flak jacket) and helmet, wear them. These "jackets" do not just prevent penetration but also disperse the shock of the bullet's impact over a larger area. In both cases, **the jacket has to be correctly fitted and done up to be effective**. Most jackets incorporate ceramic plates to afford additional protection to vital organs. Despite their weight, do not take them out.

Hollywood action movies give the wrong impression about bulletproof vests. Most are not "proof" at all—especially from high-velocity rifle fire; they just slow the passage of the bullet. The shock of being hit full-on by a high-velocity bullet causes enough blunt trauma to kill you anyway, even if the passage of the bullet through your body doesn't do so.

Low-velocity bullets on the other hand (and these include ricochets from rifle fire as well as shrapnel from exploding grenades, rockets and artillery or mortar fire) can be effectively stopped by properly fitted and properly worn body armor. Even so, the shock of being hit will knock the wind out of you and leave you with severe bruising.

If driving in an unarmored vehicle in areas where there is a known threat from direct fire—Sarajevo and the road to Tuzla in central Bosnia spring to mind—put a spare vest between you and the door on the side from which you expect to be shot at. In Bosnia, many people chose instead to drape their flak jackets over the back of the front seat—a strange practice, as the threat was rarely from behind. **Changing the vehicle's speed at unexpected moments** is highly likely to save your life, as it makes it almost impossible for a sniper to aim at you properly.

Flying into Sarajevo during the siege of 1992–95 was always an "interesting" experience. Once on the ground, the threat was mostly from indirect (artillery or mortar) fire. This

> If the situation requires body armor, consider whether you should be there.

meant a lot of running around to get under cover once disembarked from the plane. The threat when coming in to land, however, was from people shooting up at you from below. It didn't take long for passengers to realize that the best protection at that angle was afforded by sitting on a spare flak jacket or helmet. The same applies when in a car if you suspect there may be mines around.

... hand grenades

REALITY CHECK

A hand grenade was thrown over the fence into my garden in Bujumbura, Burundi, while a group of us were holding a meeting on the terrace. Luckily, the pin had not been pulled out, so it did not go off. We didn't even notice that it was a grenade until later that evening. When we did, it was treated as if it were a death threat (see page 120). In fact, according to my very relaxed guard the next morning, it was nothing more than my Tutsi neighbor's way of saying "Keep the noise down"!

It is actually quite difficult to get the safety pin out of a grenade, and it certainly can't be done with teeth. Once out, the grenade is not armed until the handle has been released. Holding a "live" grenade whose handle has been released—as I did during a break in negotiations with a Druze militiaman in a wadi on the outskirts of Beirut once—is a fairly unsettling experience, as you know that you will be blown sky-high if you drop it or hold onto it for too long.

If a fragmentation hand grenade is thrown toward you, **find cover and get behind it**. If there is none, **dive to the ground**. If it explodes in midair, the blast will throw out little pieces of metal in a more or less spherical direction and at more or less equal density. If the grenade explodes on the ground, the blast will be more cone-shaped. You can reduce the chance of one of these pieces of metal hitting you by reducing the surface area exposed to the blast. Do this by **lying on your stomach with your feet crossed and pointing toward the grenade**.

Even tiny and previously unnoticed indentations in the ground serve to deflect some of the blast upward. This means that you are less likely to be hit when lying down if the grenade is lying in an indentation. It makes no difference how close you are except that the shrapnel's lethality reduces with distance.

The explosive charge in a hand grenade is relatively small, which means that the lethal radius of a grenade is also relatively small—about 40 feet (12 meters). If you have the presence of mind, stick your fingers in your ears and keep your mouth open, as the noise of the explosion—like the noise of a gun fired indoors—is deafening.

It is possible to vary the fuse length of a grenade. The default setting for most grenades is five seconds, but this can be reduced to three or extended to seven or more by twisting the knob on the bottom. However, most people likely to chuck a grenade at you in a developing country won't know this, which means you probably have five seconds between the handle being released (when the grenade is thrown) and the

Lie on your stomach, feet crossed and pointing toward the grenade.

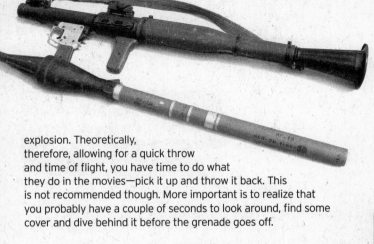

explosion. Theoretically,
therefore, allowing for a quick throw
and time of flight, you have time to do what
they do in the movies—pick it up and throw it back. This
is not recommended though. More important is to realize that
you probably have a couple of seconds to look around, find some
cover and dive behind it before the grenade goes off.

... your home being attacked

There are three keys to surviving an attack on your home:

> **Be alert to the socio-political context and the mood in the street.** In the "reality check" on page 116, streets had been emptier than normal and national colleagues had shown increasing nervousness during the preceding days. Maintain consistent dialogue with locals at work and in your neighborhood on the current situation—they can and will alert you to risks or threats.

> **Brief the house's security guards**—who are local and probably known to the attackers—**to run away when trouble appears, but to make a loud noise while doing so**. Shouting is enough, although some form of portable alarm, siren or whistle is better.

> **Err on the side of caution**, and, at the risk of seeming timid, **take shelter in the strongest internal room in the house at the first sign of trouble**. This is usually the bathroom. In fact, in many houses in Africa, the bathroom door is metal-lined, as this is designated the one "strong room." And every house should have one (see page 116).

> If gunmen have entered the building and you have not had time to gather together in a safe place such as the "strong room," **hide**. If you can't and are stranded in the open, just **stand still, keep quiet and do whatever the robbers or terrorists tell you to do**, including fetching and handing over valuables. If there is a group of you, select just one person to speak.

> **A Sudanese aid worker in Darfur was shot and killed at home in front of his family for refusing to hand over his satellite phone.**
> (*International Herald Tribune*, March 25, 2009)

REALITY CHECK

A country director with the World Food Programme still uses a leather handbag she had with her when working in a refugee camp in Ngozi, Northern Burundi, in 1996. It is peppered with shrapnel holes from an exploding RPG-7 round fired into the living room of the guesthouse where she was staying. She was saved because the other occupant of the house that evening was a former commando. He knew that anti-Western sentiment was increasing in the village and that threats were being made against the international community.

So, when he heard a commotion on the other side of the gate—caused, it later turned out, by the two security guards running away—he didn't go out to have a look. Instead, combining context with experience to act quickly, he pushed her out of the living room toward the bathroom. The grenade crashed through the window and exploded against the wall, just behind where they had been sitting moments earlier, while she was still in the corridor. I was due to stay that night too, but had been delayed in Bujumbura. When I arrived the next day, I could still smell the explosives. She, of course, had gone to work as if nothing had happened!

If you are staying for any length of time in an area where bomb blasts and robberies are not unusual—say, Baghdad or Mogadishu—it would be sensible to consider the following additional security features:

> **Cover all window glass with "anti-shard film."** It doesn't affect the view that much and may save your life. It comes as a roll of clear plastic, which can be cut to size and stuck to the inside of the glass. To stop it wrinkling and to prevent bubbles forming when fitting, spray a solution of 10 percent soap and water on the glass first, as this allows the film to slide over the glass, then smoothe with a sponge. If such film is not available, put a cross of tape diagonally, vertically and horizontally across each window pane. The purpose of both these measures is to reduce the amount of lethal glass shards flying around if the window is blown out. Closed curtains will also help absorb blast effect; the heavier the better.

> Install metal grilles that can be opened only from the inside to all windows. Fit out the designated strong room with a metal door to which bolts have been installed on both sides, i.e., the hinge side as well. (Under a sustained battering, doors with multiple bolts down the opening side often fail at the hinges.) If there is a window, make sure the grille is especially solid. But also make sure you can escape via that route if "smoked" out. Keep enough food, water and toilet paper (and a large, lidded bucket) for four people for two days' use in the room at all times.

> Store your "go kit" and first-aid kit in the strong room, so that radios (and spare batteries) with which you can call for help will always be inside. In areas with erratic water supply—the more "marginal" or underdeveloped the area, the more likely this is to be the case—experienced aid workers keep two trashcan-size containers and/or the bath constantly full with water. Really experienced people also keep chlorine tablets in the first-aid kit in case the water needs purifying.

> For external security, a low profile is the preferred option. This means no obvious signs of extra security precautions having being taken. There will, at least, be a high wall surrounding the outside area and the gate will be strong and lockable. **Hire uniformed guards to patrol inside** the compound rather than outside. A team of five is required if a 24-hour, 7-day-a-week presence of one guard is to be maintained.

> To make sure the guards stay awake, they should turn a key in a special timing device placed at the farthest point from their hut every 20 minutes. The record kept in this device needs to be ostentatiously

checked every morning; otherwise guards, however well paid and however motivated, will fall asleep on the job. If they do, they should be allowed one (very public) warning, followed by instant dismissal if they do it again. As mentioned elsewhere, these guards will run away at the first sign of trouble. They are usually unarmed, after all. Make sure that they are briefed to blow the whistle you have given them to hang around their necks (along with the time-keeping key) as they do so.

> **Keep a large dog** and have **external lights** installed (with motion sensors)—these are the best deterrents of all.

REALITY CHECK

Three young doctors from a Spanish charity came to my office in Kigali, Rwanda, one day in 1997 to announce that they were proceeding to the remote town of Rhuengheri to open up a new office. Given the recent spate of killings in that particular spot, I thought they were crazy, and said so. I explained that going to such a place was not something those on their first-ever missions should be doing—even experienced aid workers would think twice about starting up operations in such a place. But nothing would dissuade them.

Three days later, news came through that all three had been shot dead during an attempted robbery of their new home. It later became clear that they had not followed any of the advice given to them (as outlined in this book) and had even opened the outside gate to the assailants themselves, having not seen fit to hire local security guards. Naive, foolish or brave? You decide. For my part, I was more angry than sad at such senseless loss of life and have tried ever since to make sure that people with limited field experience listen to the advice of their more experienced colleagues.

... **bomb threats**

REALITY CHECK

You can defend yourself from a truck bomb. I first came across the concept as operations officer for the British force in Lebanon in 1983. We had received a warning from one of the militias fighting for control of Beirut that a truck bomb was targeted at the base of one of the international forces. A few hours later, our small and rather exposed peacekeeping force had constructed a solid obstacle of mounds of earth on both approach roads with a bulldozer "borrowed" from a nearby building site, making it impossible for a vehicle to approach the base at any speed. The intelligence turned out to be correct, and you may still remember the carnage that followed when a truck bomb was driven right into the U.S. Marine compound not far away, collapsing the building and killing over 230 Marines. They had not yet constructed any obstacles, making them an easier target than us.

   This lesson had been forgotten twenty years later when twenty-three colleagues and friends lost their lives—most of them from injuries sustained by flying glass—when a truck bomb was driven into the UN Canal Hotel in Baghdad, where I had my office. By pure chance, I was not in the building at the time.

There is little defense from an individual suicide bomber, except to **vary your routine, take a different route to work each day and stagger your times of departure** if you live in a high-risk part of the world. Avoid high-value targets if possible, as well as congested areas and major traffic jams, especially if they are due to security checkpoints.

To minimize the risk of premeditated attack, be predictably unpredictable.

If a bomb threat is made or a suspicious package found, **evacuate the building and move a safe distance away** (300 yards). As the "reality check" on page 116 demonstrates, **avoid passing windows**, even if they have been covered with plastic anti-shard film (see page 117). Whatever you do, **do not look for or move the suspect device**. If a suspicious letter or package is discovered, it should be

119

put down gently. Do not put anything on top of it, and do not put it in water.

Parcel bombs and letter bombs have similar characteristics, and can usually be distinguished by being oil-stained, heavier at one end than the other, wrapped in excessive tape or having visible wires. According to a bomb-disposal friend, they don't "tick."

If you receive a bomb threat by telephone, the procedures outlined below might be appropriate, depending on the circumstances. However, as with death threats (see next section), most bomb threats are hoaxes. But treat them as real and urgent until the area has been searched and the security services have pronounced it to be clear.

There have been cases where slow reactions to bomb warnings have led to additional deaths and injuries. Don't hang up. Instead, record the exact wording of the threat, if you can, and ask questions of the caller, such as:

> Where is the bomb right now?
> When is it going to explode?
> What does it look like?

If possible, also make a note of:

> background noises (street noises, house noises, music, etc.)
> whether it sounds like a local, long-distance or international call
> the accent of the caller
> the time, date, duration and number called

... death threats

REALITY CHECK

Working in areas of armed conflict lays everyone open to accusations of aiding one side or another, despite all efforts to remain neutral and independent. Many UN agency staff, journalists and NGO workers received death threats in Burundi in 1995. I was among them.

Death threats are not all that uncommon and constitute the first-line method of intimidation. Normally delivered anonymously over the phone with few words and much heavy breathing, but sometimes by letter and increasingly via badly misspelled email, such threats usually come from the friends or family of disgruntled staff, paramilitary gang members who are unhappy at you "bearing witness" to their activities or political activists. However "field" you are, they are invariably unnerving. Keep copies of written threats and even record those received over the phone if you can and they are a regular occurrence.

Do not overreact to a death threat.

Each and every threat should be taken extremely seriously even though they are highly unlikely to be followed through. You do not need to overreact to a single threat. As a rule of thumb, the risk rises proportionately with the frequency of threats. Either way, **each threat should be logged and reported to the local authorities**. Let your organization know too, and make sure they inform the local UN security team, who can usually furnish information on how common such a threat is and if others are receiving the same. Both you and your organization should seek written and formal confirmation from the local authorities that they are taking your protection seriously. **When these authorities suggest they can "no longer guarantee your safety," it is time to consider leaving.**

In the meantime, take the following precautions:

> **Change your cell telephone number.**

> **Randomize your routine activities** by altering departure times and routes to work.

> **Sleep over with friends or book into a hotel on random nights.**

> **Tell your friends what is going on** so that each of them knows you will call them when you are worried. Make sure that they know who, in turn, to call should they receive a frantic call from you one night.

> **Ensure that those guarding your property know what to do if a forced entry is attempted.** Expecting locals to guard you with their lives is unrealistic. In all likelihood, they will run away at the first sign of genuine trouble. At least make sure they make a noise when doing so. Blowing a whistle or activating a rape alarm is the best you can expect.

> Ensure that your safe room is actually safe (i.e., it has a metal door and a window with solid bolts and hinges) and stocked with food and water as well as radio battery recharging facilities.

... kidnapping and hostage negotiations

REALITY CHECK

Alan Johnston, a BBC journalist, was kidnapped in Gaza in March 2007 and held for almost four months. This is what he had to say about his ordeal: "I knew that kidnap victims suffered worst when they felt the world had forgotten them. Hearing my name in snatches of news on the guards' radio were inspirational and kept me going. I remember listening to messages from Terry Waite [who had been held hostage in Beirut for nearly four years] in which he urged me to live each day as it came and not to build up hopes, as the impact of them being dashed could be devastating. I was told I was being released on a number of occasions only for this to be a hoax. I learned quickly that in 'Hotel Jihad' all dawns were false. I kept going by thinking how fortunate I was in comparison with terminal cancer patients, who act with such dignity when told they are going to die. I was lucky compared to them. I kept telling myself that I did not have death to look forward to but I was preparing myself for life to begin again. I kept telling myself that I have not been killed, I have not been tortured and the food's okay. That's a start. I built from there."

According to a clinical psychologist who has counseled tsunami victims as well as Iraq War veterans, "the experience [Alan Johnston] went through has been very disorientating. But, once released, his initial delight will quickly give way to feelings of being overloaded, because he has been without proper communication and conversation for so long. He will probably suffer flashbacks, nightmares, insomnia, anxiety attacks and hyper-vigilance for the next four to six weeks, and would benefit from immediate psychological debriefing with a specialist counsellor. But human beings are incredibly resilient and draw on inner resources they never knew they had. This is one of the positives."

Your abductors will initially threaten you or attempt to humiliate you. But bear in mind that the longer you are held, the less likely it is that you will be killed.

Avoid attention-seeking behavior and note that hostage-takers are nervous too. If you can, **hide your passport. If you are English-speaking, pretend to be Irish or Canadian**, as these are widely perceived to be two more or less "neutral" countries. If capture is inevitable, **accept it and follow instructions**. Once captured, **prepare mentally for a long wait** (think in terms of months), meanwhile doing as much of the following as you can remember:

> eat food that is given to you, even if it is unpalatable

> adopt a realistic attitude of discreet skepticism toward information passed on to you by your captors

> systematically occupy your mind with constructive and positive thoughts

> plan a daily program of activity, including daily physical exercise, and adhere to it

> try to keep an accurate record of time, even if your watch is taken away from you

> take advantage of any comforts or privileges offered to you by your captors, like books, newspapers or access to the radio—ask for them

> keep as clean as circumstances permit—ask for adequate bathing and toilet facilities

> develop, if possible, a good rapport with your captors and try to earn their respect

Do not:

> antagonize your captors unnecessarily—they have you in their power

> permit yourself to be drawn into conversations about controversial subjects such as politics and religious beliefs

> allow yourself to become either depressed or over-optimistic

> commit physical violence or verbal aggression

> attempt to escape

> believe it when you are told that you have been abandoned by your organization and by your family

The longer you are held, the less likely you are to be killed.

Family and friends must realize that former hostages feel the need to withdraw some days after their release. It can be upsetting, but they should try to understand (see **coming home** section).

Avoid all talk of religion.

Although hostage situations can vary greatly, based on the motivations of the hostage taker and the exact circumstances surrounding the incident, there are some basic facts that apply to all hostage situations:

> **Hostage takers want something.** This can be as simple as money and safe passage to another country, or it can involve complicated political goals.

> **The target of the hostage taker is not the hostage;** it is some third party (a person, a company or a government) that can provide whatever it is the hostage taker wants.

> **Hostages are bargaining chips.** They may have symbolic value but the hostages themselves could be anyone.

Resolution of hostage situations move through several distinct phases:

> **Initial phase:** this phase is violent and brief and lasts as long as it takes for the hostage takers to make their assault and subdue the hostages. The end of this phase is often marked by the presentation of the hostage takers' demands.

> **Negotiation or "stand-off" phase:** at this point, law-enforcement officials and/or security advisers are on the scene, and the demands have probably been received. This phase can last weeks or months, during which time a lot is happening in terms of the relationships developing between everyone involved. The negotiator's job boils down to manipulating those relationships in a way that results in a peaceful ending. The new trend, especially in the Afghanistan/Pakistan border areas, is for hostages to be relocated many times during this phase as the original kidnappers sell the hostages on to other groups who may have different demands and different political agendas.

> **Termination phase:** this is the brief, sometimes violent, final phase.

Hostage takers intend from the beginning to trade the lives of their hostages for whatever specific goals they want to achieve. Terrorist groups may also have goals that they will achieve regardless of the outcome: e.g., destabilizing the target of their attack and attracting attention to their cause.

At the beginning of a hostage crisis, the hostage takers' demands are often unreasonable. They might ask for huge sums of money or for the release of fellow terrorists from jails. Of course, the negotiator can't just give them anything they ask for, even if it would mean the safety of the hostages. The policies of any nations involved, the ability to actually acquire the items being demanded and the need to consult with the situation commander and high-ranking political officials all limit what a negotiator can offer to hostage takers. Plus if anyone who took hostages immediately had all of his or her demands granted, the world would face one hostage crisis after another.

However, a negotiator can "chip away" at the situation by offering minor concessions, such as food and water, promises of transportation and media coverage. In return, the hostage takers can trade some of the hostages or some of their weapons, or agree to downgrade some of their demands. By continuing this process, the negotiator can gradually undermine the hostage takers' position.

Most countries and organizations have official policies regarding negotiating with terrorists. However, these policies shift with time, and they tend to be flexible, depending on the situation. If the hostages are children or important political officials, even the most hardline nonnegotiating government might make an exception. In many cases, secret deals are made that allow the government to accept demands and save the hostages but maintain their public hard-line stance against giving in to terrorists' demands. Such deals are usually carried out by a third party so that the government concerned can maintain "plausible deniability."

Israel, the United States, the U.K. and Russia are all nations that have a reputation for having strict nonnegotiation policies. However, every policy is open to exception.

Although refusing to negotiate with terrorists is often a politically popular idea (no one wants to "give in" to terrorists), it can be disastrous. Even if a government has no intention of granting demands, the process of negotiating itself is vital to achieving a peaceful resolution. Two of the most horrific hostage incidents in history ended in tragedy in large part due to Russia's outright refusal to negotiate with Muslim Chechen separatists when further negotiations might have reduced the number of casualties.

... **arrest**

One freezing March morning in 1992, while working for the EC Monitor Mission in former Yugoslavia, I found myself discussing ceasefire options with a bunch of Serb generals in the town of Knin, the self-proclaimed capital of a disputed part of an area called Krajina.

Such discussions always seemed to take place in icy bombed-out basements, and proceeded only after the consumption of copious amounts of a locally distilled plum brandy called *slivovica*. It was also de rigueur to smoke. And so it was, with a cigarette stuffed between gloved fingers, drunk and unable to see my interlocutors across the table through the cigar smoke, that I got myself arrested.

Questioning was innocuous at first: "Where are you from?" "England," I said. "What are you doing here?" "Trying to see if you and the Croats can come to some settlement over your land dispute near Zadar [a Croat coastal town to the west] without killing more of each other," I replied. "Who do you work for?" I paused before answering and, thinking that it might increase my credibility, I truthfully said, "The British Foreign Office." Well, that was it. A *slivovica*-induced diatribe against the evils of the Croatian Ushtase (the Nazi puppet regime during the Second World War) followed and I was handcuffed and thrown in a police cell. After a long, cold and lonely twenty-four hours protesting that I was a "diplomat"—which was only half true—I was eventually bundled into a small car and driven north through the beautiful snowy lakes of Plitvica National Park to be handed over to my colleagues at Karlovac in Croatia.

As a footnote to this story, I went back about six months later to see if something further could be done to stop the fighting, which had, if anything, intensified since my previous visit. This time, the Serb paramilitaries were different and didn't recognize me. When asked where I was from, for some reason I said "Scotland" instead of "England." The response could not have been more different—or more welcoming. "Ah, a Scotsman!" they cried. "So, my friend, you understand us. You understand the mountains, the drinking, the clan . . . but above all"—at this, my mug was filled with an enormous quantity of yet more *slivovica* while I was bear-hugged by a very large man with a bushy black beard—"you understand secession!"

Perhaps unsurprisingly, I always say I am from Scotland now, even though I am only half Scots and live in England, and am always well treated when I do. This applied even when I had to arrest myself after landing my paraglider on a remote roadside in Tanzania… the arresting officer was so large that his small motorbike could not make it up the Ngara escarpment with both of us on it. So he flagged down a passing car and I followed him to the police station on his motorbike.

More often than not, foreign police and intelligence agencies detain people for no other reason than mere suspicion or curiosity. If this happens to you, the best option is to exercise good judgment and be professional in your demeanor. It would be as well to remember the following advice too:

> **Ask to contact the nearest embassy** or consulate representing your country. As a citizen of another country, you have this right, but that does not mean that your hosts will allow you to exercise it. If they refuse or just ignore you, continue to make the request periodically until they accede.

> Stay calm, maintain your dignity and **do not do anything to provoke** the arresting officer(s).

> **Do not admit anything or volunteer any information.**

> **Do not sign anything.** Often, part of the detention procedure is to ask or tell the detainee to sign a written report. Decline politely until such time as the document is examined by an attorney or an embassy/consulate representative.

> Do not accept anyone at face value. When the representative from the embassy or consulate arrives, **request some identification before discussing your situation**.

> Do not fall for the ruse of helping those who are detaining you in return for your release and do not sell yourself out by agreeing to anything. If they will not take no for an answer, do not make a firm commitment or sign anything. Tell them that you will think it over and let them know.

If you are arrested, say little and sign nothing without a lawyer or embassy representative present.

... **hotels and guesthouses**

Choose where you stay with care. As the "reality check" above points out, not all hotels are the same, although they might look as if they have the same levels of security in their marketing material. Avoid those being used by delegations of U.S. officials or business groups, especially in Islamic countries.

Select a room on the second to eighth floor—preferably on the second or third floor (i.e., not the ground floor)—this is high enough not to tempt opportunistic thieves in the street yet low enough to be reached by mobile fire ladders (at least in larger cities with adequate fire services). You will probably break your legs if you are forced to jump from any higher than three floors above the ground. Avoid rooms that open onto external corridors or face onto the street if prone to attack (as in Kabul, for example). If in an area of seismic instability, avoid buildings of between three and eight stories—these are statistically the most liable to collapse (see **earthquakes** section).

Once in your hotel or guesthouse, **don't open your door to anyone you don't know**. Call reception to check names/identifications. Keep windows and balcony doors locked, and keep the curtains drawn at night.

If you choose to eat in or near the hotel lobby, don't sit at the front but near the rear entrance and away from glass windows.

In an elevator, stand near the control panel. If threatened, hit the alarm button and press as many buttons as you can reach so that the elevator will stop at the next floor. If someone gets in that you don't like the look of, stop the elevator at the next available floor and get out.

Don't go for a walk at night around the hotel on your own, and, if you do, don't take shortcuts through isolated or dark areas. **Carry only the cash that you need and divide it between different pockets.** Emergency cash should be safely tucked into your money belt.

Burglars and rapists are not nearly as common in remoter guesthouses and hostels as the media would have you believe. Yet fear of attack when sleeping, especially among women, remains a major concern for all who work or travel abroad. Fire, quite rightly, is also a major concern—fire escapes are a luxury not normally found in developing countries. **A personal fire alarm** is therefore a sound investment. Such an alarm can also double as a burglar and rape alarm. Arm it and hang it on the top of the door. It will go off if the door is opened or if it detects smoke (smoke rises, so the higher it is placed, the better).

Place a wedge-shaped (preferably rubber) **doorstop under the door** to make forced entry difficult. Do this whether or not the door appears to be lockable. This will buy enough time for you to beat a hasty exit through the window if someone is trying to force their way in (extremely unusual, this).

> **Pack a rubber door wedge.**

If you insist on having the window open, **attach a couple of empty cans or bottles to some string**, leave them standing on the windowsill, one on either side of the opening, and stretch the string between the two across the window a few inches above the lintel. They will fall with a clatter if anyone attempts entry, and nine times out of ten the intruder will run away when faced with such noise.

Many small hotels and guesthouses in developing countries argue that bars across the windows or some other form of window lock are essential for your security. If you are unsure about your escape route in the event of a fire, and evacuation through the window appears to be the only viable option, either insist on having them removed or stay somewhere else.

Plan your evacuation route before you go to sleep—smoke-filled

Smoke rises.
Keep your mouth at floor level.

corridors are notoriously difficult to navigate. If you are faced with a smoke-filled corridor, **crawl down it with your nose and mouth as close to the floor as possible**. Remember, smoke rises. If you are trapped, read on . . .

. . . escaping a burning building

REALITY CHECK

A couple, Pike and Doyle, were staying at a Mumbai hotel in November 2008 when it became the target of terrorist attack and was set ablaze. Realizing that there was no escape except through the window, they made a makeshift rope out of sheets and curtains. Pike used a marble table to smash through the window. He volunteered to go first to make sure the rope was strong enough to support their weight.

"We threw the rope out of the window and it was not bad, given that it was 60 feet to the ground. But clearly I never did my Boy Scout knot badge because my knots were rubbish," Pike said.

Kissing Doyle and telling her he loved her, he climbed out of the window.

"I put all my weight on the rope and the last thing I remember was falling. I remember looking up and seeing the ledge going away and the rope falling down with me. The next thing I remember I was on the ground looking at the bone shards sticking out of my wrist." He survived, although he also sustained a broken back. Doyle was rescued minutes later by a fire-brigade ladder.

If fire is raging in the corridor outside, the door handle will be too hot to touch. If this is the case, **don't open the door**—many people are fatally injured by the sudden "blast" of flame that roars in.

If you are trapped in a burning building and have to escape through the window, you have little option but to **make a rope from the sheets and/or curtains** to climb down. (Don't use bath towels as the weft and weave is too loose to take the weight of a body.)

Having first placed wet towels at the foot of the door to prevent ingress of smoke, **rip all sheets into 18-inch(45-cm)-wide strips and tie them together lengthways** by means of a reef knot (see **tying knots** section). A granny knot is likely to come undone, as the story above seems to confirm! Run the bath. This is not for you to get in, it's to **soak the rope**.

REALITY CHECK

According to a policeman friend of mine, it's surprising how many people are found dead in the bath after a hotel fire. "Evidently," he says, "they get in to escape the heat but forget that this is the method we use for cooking lobsters . . . !"

Once the rope is wet, tie one end to something solid such as pipework. One leg of the bed will do as an alternative—loop the rope around two legs if it is long enough. The trick then is to **twist the rope** as much as possible, as the additional friction between the fibers will increase the tensile strength of the knots and the material—it will unravel as you climb down, but not completely. If you tie something heavy to the end, it will unravel less.

Throw the mattresses out of the window first, as these will help cushion the impact if you fall. **Wrap an article of clothing around your head** as an improvised helmet.

Throw the rope out, then climb out and **slide down one at a time** as fast as you can. Apart from stopping your hands being burned from the friction, the wetness of the rope will also make it stronger as well as reducing the chance of it catching fire. If there are a lot of you, place a coat under the rope at the point where it is likely to chafe against the windowsill.

Given the limited number of sheets and curtain material likely to be available, it is unlikely that the rope will extend more than five

stories. If, having reached
the end, you are still above
the ground, just let go. Keep
your legs together and absorb
the shock of hitting the ground by
"folding" the legs and rolling as parachutists sometimes do.
Humans can normally survive a jump of three stories. And breaking
your legs is better than being suffocated or burned alive.

> **A rope of wet and twisted bed sheets if properly tied will bear a man's weight.**

... a fight

One way to avoid getting hurt in an ugly confrontation is what
George W. Bush used to call "anticipated retaliation"—better known
as the "pre-emptive strike." The best way to immobilize a potential
assailant before he (it is unlikely to be a "she") hits you is to **deliver a
short, sharp punch upward into the bottom of the rib cage**. This will
"wind" him, rendering him unable to catch his breath for a while. It is
possible to run away in this "breathing space." Better still, run away
before he gets in range.

Just as successful (if you hit the target) is to aim a "karate chop" with
the side of your hand to the throat. Pretend to be making friends
(easier if you are female) and then **hit the assailant's Adam's apple
as hard as you can**. You can also try poking his eyes with fingers
spread into a V shape or **kneeing the potential attacker as hard as
you can in the groin**. This is the defense tactic of choice for most
women.

If you insist on "punching" the assailant, do so using your elbow or
heel of your hand. Use of a clenched fist leaves you with very sore, if
not broken, knuckles.

If you prefer passivity, **turn sideways to absorb any body blow. For a
blow aimed at the head, move into
it if you can as this will dissipate
the force**, while attempting to
deflect the blow with your arm.

If the attacker has a knife or gun,
don't resist but maintain eye

> **When being robbed, do not resist. Pass over your valuables slowly and deliberately.**

contact, talk to him and offer to pass over your valuables, starting with your watch.

Don't make any sudden movements as this may provoke the attacker unnecessarily. He is, after all, probably just as high on adrenaline as you at this moment.

... **a riot**

Personal Security

The best course is not to "mix it" with a rioting mob in the first place. However, if you are inadvertently caught up in a riot, as I was, the old adage "if you can't beat 'em, join 'em" holds true. Blend in. **The best way to survive a riot is to become one of the rioters.** You have a better chance of escaping from the police unscathed than from a mob.

If a riot is taking place outside, **stay indoors, stay informed and don't leave** unless you have to. **Keep in constant touch** (by phone or radio) with friends farther away, and **make a plan of escape in case you have to leave in a hurry**. If you do decide to leave, **stick together and have a destination agreed upon beforehand. Walk. Don't attract attention by running, and keep moving. Stay away from main streets. Avoid everyone else. Drink plenty of water and eat something before setting off**—you won't know where your next meal is coming from. Have a street map handy, and keep track of where the police/rioters are from radio reports. **Remove any watches or jewelry before you go.** Wear shoes that you can run in and that are sturdy enough to protect your feet from broken glass.

If you expect to run into tear gas, **wear something waterproof** with tight cuffs and a collar. Goggles would also be helpful if you have them—but so would a gas mask! A bandana soaked in lime juice to breathe through, or lemon or lime slices to suck on, will help in a pinch. If you're caught in a chemical attack, **pay attention to which way the smoke from the tear gas is blowing and try to stay away from it**—upwind if possible. Don't pick up a smoking tear-gas canister as it is hot and will burn you; kick it away instead.

If you are teargassed you will be able to tell. The effects last for twenty minutes or so, and include running nose, running eyes and shortness of breath. Tear gas is designed to temporarily incapacitate, not maim, so you will recover—though it doesn't feel like it at the time: snot from your nose is running everywhere, you can't see, and breathing is both painful and difficult. Try to avoid rubbing the tear gas around your body or onto others. Use cold water to wash your skin. Wash out your eyes by pouring water from the inside corner to the outside corner.

The spray from a water cannon will knock you over. But if you have gotten that close to the security services you have been doing something wrong. The water is also often mixed with a chemical irritant and/or indelible dye so that you can be identified later.

Firing live ammunition into a crowd is supposedly a control measure of last resort. However, some countries, particularly those run by military dictatorships or where the police have become a law unto themselves, are not squeamish when it comes to employing such drastic tactics. If you hear the distinctive *crack* and *thump* of live rounds being fired, whether incoming, outgoing or over your head, it is time to get out of the line of sight fast.

Chapter 5

Getting There

How to deal with ...

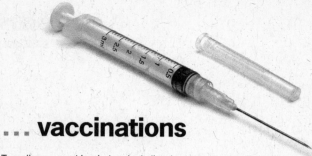

... **vaccinations**

Traveling or working in tropical climates exposes you to bugs and diseases that your body will not have encountered before and for which you will have no natural immunity. Consult a physician well before departure to make sure your vaccinations are relevant and up-to-date as some require more than one inoculation some weeks apart.

Make sure you travel with your vaccination record, as many countries will not allow you to enter without proof that you have had certain inoculations—particularly yellow fever. **At a minimum, you should be current for:**

> **Hepatitis-A**: an RNA virus transmitted through the faeco-oral route (i.e., via contaminated fingers) that turns the patient yellow. It is generally a nonlife-threatening condition but leaves sufferers feeling lethargic for up to six months. Because the virus infects the liver, alcohol cannot be consumed during recovery—which many patients describe as worse than the disease itself.

> **Hepatitis-B**: another of the range of viral diseases that affect the liver. It can cause long-term health problems as well as death in certain patients. About 10 percent of infected adults will later develop some of the more significant complications from this disease, including cirrhosis and liver cancer.

> **Typhoid**: a bacterial disease transmitted through contaminated food and water. The risk of contracting typhoid is thought to be in the region of 1:5,000 for the international traveler to the tropics. Typically the disease presents with fever and severe headaches. Despite the high fever, many patients show a characteristic slowing of the heart rate. Patients may also have either constipation or pea-colored diarrhea (common in both salmonella and shigella infections). It can be treated with ciprofloxacin.

> **Yellow fever**: a flavivirus carried from one animal to another by mosquitoes. The "yellow" in the name is explained by the jaundice affecting some patients. There is no specific treatment for yellow fever. Dehydration and fever can be corrected with oral rehydration salts and acetaminophen. Any superimposed bacterial infection should be treated with an appropriate antibiotic. There are two disease phases. While some infections have no symptoms whatsoever, the first "acute" phase is normally characterized by fever, muscle pain (with prominent backache), headache, shivers, loss of appetite, nausea and/or vomiting. Often, the high fever is paradoxically associated with a slow pulse. After three to four days, most patients improve and their symptoms disappear. However, 15 percent enter the second "toxic" phase within twenty-four hours. Half of the patients in the toxic phase die within ten to fourteen days. The remainder recover without significant organ damage.

> **Meningococcal meningitis**: a bacterial disease characterized by the sudden onset of intense headache, fever, nausea, vomiting, photophobia and stiff neck. Neurological signs include lethargy, delirium, coma and/or convulsions. The fatality rate is between 5 and 15 percent if diagnosed early and given adequate therapy but may exceed 50 percent in the absence of treatment. It should therefore always be viewed as a medical emergency. Admission to a hospital or health center is necessary, where a lumbar puncture will be required to confirm diagnosis. Oily chloramphenicol is often the drug of choice in areas with limited health facilities. You should make sure you are given the quadrivalent vaccine for serogroups A, C, W 135 and Y.

If you have not been revaccinated against these common diseases in the past ten years, you should also have "booster" shots for the following (you have probably forgotten they existed, but these diseases remain among the largest causes of avoidable death around the world):

> **Diphtheria**: in many countries the diphtheria vaccine is combined with pertussis (whooping cough) and tetanus. It was doubtless given to you on three occasions during the first six months of life.

> **Tetanus**: a potentially fatal infection caused by a bacterium called *Clostridium tetani* that attacks the muscles and nervous system. The bacteria live in the soil and dirt and get into your body through a cut or a wound in the skin. The vaccine is normally part of the combined diphtheria/tetanus/pertussis/polio/hemophilus influenzae-b

vaccine that is given as part of routine childhood immunization programs nowadays. If you completed the course as a child, you should have lifelong immunity. However, have a booster if your last shot was over ten years ago.

> **Measles**: still one of the biggest killers of children in the world. The vaccine is a live, attenuated (weakened) strain of the measles virus. It is routinely given as part of the MMR vaccine, which protects against measles, mumps and rubella (German measles).

> **Tuberculosis**: a highly transmissible but perfectly curable disease caused by various types of *Mycobacterium*. At least one-third of the human population is infected, although 90 percent of the disease is confined to Africa, Central and South America and Asia. A prolonged course of treatment is required. I contracted one of the many different forms while working in the TB clinics of Albania, and I'm still here.

> **Polio**: a water-borne viral disease, which WHO is still trying to eradicate as it did smallpox. There are two main vaccines, both of which work very well. The Sabin version is given as drops (sometimes on a sugar cube to hide the bitter taste) and the Salk version is given by injection. In patients with progressive disease, paralysis may develop. This is flaccid (floppy) and typically asymmetric with only one side of the body involved. In patients with higher infection, full paralysis may develop with respiratory failure and rapid death. There is no specific treatment.

Depending on where you are going, you should also consider being vaccinated against:

> **Rabies**: a fatal viral infection for which there is no treatment once symptoms become evident—usually between three weeks and three months after being bitten. Only one person in six ever develops symptoms, but once visible symptoms have developed, the mortality rate is almost 100 percent. Very few people have been known to survive a rabies infection, which is why it is rightly feared. Death results from respiratory paralysis. You need three injections over a three-week period. Contrary to popular belief, these injections are quite "normal," not the painful jabs into the stomach of the past.

> **Cholera**: an acute intestinal infection caused by one of the many different *Vibrio cholerae* bacteria. Outbreaks, caused by contaminated water supply, spread rapidly. The copious, painless, watery diarrhea that results can quickly lead to severe dehydration and death if treatment is not promptly given. Vomiting also occurs in most patients.

Most cases can be treated adequately by administering oral rehydration salts, although more severe cases will need IV infusion and antibiotics specific to the infecting strain of *Vibrio*. There are two oral cholera vaccines that provide high-level protection for several months against certain strains. However, the chances are that if you do become infected it will be by a different strain against which the vaccine has no effect. The vaccine also gives a false sense of security.

> **Japanese encephalitis**: a viral disease transmitted by female *Culex* mosquitoes that kills between 10 and 40 percent of those who contract it. It is found mainly in Southeast Asia. Early gastrointestinal symptoms are followed by seizures and paralysis as the virus affects the patient's brain tissue. The risk of contracting this deadly disease is approximately 1:5,000 for those living in rural areas for more than one month in endemic countries. This is particularly the case between May and September in Southeast Asia or between July and December in north India, Pakistan and Bangladesh. There is a dead vaccine against the disease, which should be used if going to these places. The vaccine is given on three occasions (days 0, 7–14, 28), which should confer between two and three years of immunity.

There is currently no vaccine for **malaria**, and there are two schools of thought about alternative methods of malaria prevention. If you are going abroad for only a few weeks, especially if going to areas where *falciparum* (cerebral) malaria is endemic, doctors advise taking antimalarial tablets. The course requires a daily dose and starts before you depart and continues after your return. Aid workers going abroad for months or years usually don't take antimalarials, as there can be complicating side effects such as dizziness and hallucinations. Supply is also likely to be interrupted. Instead, they make every effort not to get bitten by mosquitoes, the vector for the *Plasmodium* parasites, in the first place. They do this by covering bare arms and legs in the evening, when the *Anopheles* mosquito comes looking for a blood-meal, and slapping liberal doses of "mozzie repellent" onto the back of the neck, temples, hands, wrists, feet and ankles. And by sleeping under securely fastened insecticide-treated bed nets (see **high fever** section).

For country-specific information, I have found the Irish Tropical Medical Bureau's website very useful: www.tmb.ie.

... **obtaining a visa**

Deployment of humanitarian personnel to disaster zones is frequently delayed due to visa and/or passport problems. Experienced aid workers have two passports, one of which is likely to be "in for a visa" at any one time. If you don't want to waste two half-days standing in line in some dingy basement consular section on the other side of town, it is worth bearing in mind the following—especially as visa restrictions are tightening up around the world:

> You usually need at least one blank page in your passport (in some cases, two facing each other) in addition to the page required for the visa you are now applying for.

> The expiration date of your passport should be more than six months from your date of travel.

> Don't arrive for your flight home without some hard currency in small denominations on you, as many less developed countries charge an exit tax that must be paid in the exact amount in hard currency.

> Many countries give you the option to pay for the visa on arrival. This can be cheaper than getting one from the embassy, though there could be long lines at the border and you run a higher risk of being refused entry. Usually, such visas must be paid for in hard currency (normally U.S. dollars or euros). In general, it is advisable to obtain a visa before reaching the border, for your own peace of mind.

> Often, visas can only be applied for and collected from consular sections at limited times and on limited days. Check with the embassy concerned (by phone—website information, especially for smaller countries, is often out-of-date) before setting off.

> Get to the embassy early, as long lines can form very quickly even for less well-known destinations.

> Most embassies refuse credit cards and personal checks.

> It is sometimes possible to apply by mail, although this method takes longer. Application forms can be downloaded from several embassy websites. You'll usually need to send your passport and include a self-addressed, stamped envelope (either by registered mail or special delivery for safe return).

> If you don't want to go it alone, there are many visa agencies ready to do the legwork—at a price. In addition to the visa fee itself, expect to pay a fee for the service plus special delivery charges. Fees are based on how difficult the visa is to procure, so they can vary. This might seem a luxury, but it compares favorably against the time and money it takes to travel to the embassy in question, stand in line for your application to be processed and then to repeat the exercise when collecting the visa in person. Most aid agency personnel prefer this route, as it frees up time to plan and prepare for what is bound to be an arduous trip.

> Many countries require you to register at the local police station within five days of arrival.

... **packing light**

We all tend to take too much when going abroad. Be ruthless when packing. One medium-size suitcase (or backpack, depending on how mobile you intend to be) and one carry-on bag is all that is needed. Both should be fitted with wheels and at least one should be lockable and constructed of material which cannot be cut with a knife. Most airlines will let you carry on a daypack, too, into which other bits and pieces needed for traveling and precious electrical items such as iPods, phones and laptops go. This will double as your briefcase later.

The trick is to pack multiuse clothing and accessories. What's needed is outlined in detail at the back of the book. In essence, wear field clothes when traveling, including the boots and cold-weather stuff if you're going somewhere cold. Restrict yourself to another set of field clothes, three sets of underwear, two sets of off-duty clothes (but only one pair of shoes) that can be "mixed and matched," at least one of which can be both casual and formal, two white T-shirts, and a jacket (plus tie for men). The more crease-proof such clothing is, the better.

For men, shaving kits can be reduced to a toothbrush (with half the handle broken off), a small tube of toothpaste, a razor (plus one spare blade loose), a small bar of antibacterial soap (in a waterproof container), roll-on underarm deodorant, nail clippers, tweezers and a universal bath plug. If you use a scented oil instead of the soap to shave, you won't need aftershave.

Women, of course, need slightly more than this. Absolutely essential appears to be an enormous volume of makeup crammed into a multitude of multicolored bags with bursting zipper, then another stuffed full of cheap jewelry. To this is added a hair dryer at the very least. As a man, I have never understood the need for such vast quantities of sprays, creams, gels and the instruments of torture with which they are applied.

If sport is your thing, shorts and running shoes will be needed, too. If you're really sharp, the shorts can double as your swimming trunks while a bikini can double as underwear (though not the other way around).

... **setting off**

There is nothing more irritating or worrying when abroad than losing your passport, return air ticket, credit cards or yellow-fever vaccination certificate—all of which are needed when traveling. Before setting off, make sure that you **email scanned copies of all your important documents to yourself**, and send a copy to a loved one back home and someone you know in the country you are visiting. These include:

> airline e-ticket
> passport
> passport photo
> driving license
> visa
> work and/or residence permit (if required)
> insurance details
> vaccination record
> yellow-fever certificate (in addition to the more general vaccination record)
> security in the field certificate (if in the UN)

> health certificate (including blood group)
> a list of important telephone numbers back home (including credit-card cancellation)
> credit-card details
> details of next of kin

Even in this day and age, however, hard photocopies remain useful. Keep three photocopies of your passport and visa in three separate places, one of which should be on your person at all times, another in your office (if you have one) and another with a friend.

Have at least eight passport photographs with you.

Some countries allow their citizens to hold two passports. If you can, you should. Visas from one country can infuriate another (Israel and the Occupied Palestinian Territories spring to mind) so are best put in separate

Email scanned copies of important documents to yourself.

passports. Also, hide one with a friend in case you lose the main one, as there is nothing more boring than having to explain to a skeptical and self-important consular official why you need an emergency passport (which will not in any case get you where you want to go— only home).

Put spare cash in a strong (not fabric) lockable suitcase and attach the suitcase to an immovable object with a wire cable and/ or a portable multipurpose alarm. This deters opportunistic theft, especially in a hotel or guesthouse, where a local walking out with an expensive suitcase tends to arouse suspicion.

A multipurpose alarm incorporates an LED flashlight (with strobe and ambient light facility) with a rape, smoke and theft alarm. This is probably the best investment in personal security you will ever make.

Keep US$300 in new denomination (post-2003) 50-dollar bills in a money belt around your waist (a belt, not a pouch).

It might seem a bit morbid, **but make sure your will is up-to-date** and properly witnessed by someone who is not a beneficiary. Also make sure that someone close to you knows where to find both it and details of all your assets. Add your email and/or Facebook password so that this person can use your list to let all your friends know what has happened.

If you are traveling to a disaster zone for a humanitarian aid agency, it is quite normal to find yourself lumbered with 175 pounds of "essential equipment" just as you set off to the airport. If this happens to you, **make sure you get a letter on the organization's letterhead explaining what you are flying out to do and including a polite request to allow the overweight baggage to go for free** (but note that, if contacted in advance, many major airlines will allow excess baggage allowance to those traveling on humanitarian missions). At check-in, shamelessly brandish this letter. If the handler on duty is less than impressed, ask to see the airline's duty manager. In three out of four of the times I have tried this, not only does the overweight baggage go for free but, without asking, I have also been given an upgrade.

If you are not lucky enough to wangle an upgrade, one way of getting more than one seat in a row is to make sure you are the very last person to board the aircraft—and I mean as the doors are closing. Having booked your seat toward the back (do this online 24 hours prior to departure), walk toward it scanning for empty seats as you go. If you see some vacant, sit in the middle of them (if there are three or more together) as if that was your designated seat all along.

If your checked baggage is not locked and one of those cellophane bag-wrapping services is available, use it. This is particularly important on internal flights in less developed countries where foreigners' bags are easily spotted by greedy baggage handlers. A colleague flying with me to Astana from Almaty in Kazakhstan arrived without his boots because he wanted to save two dollars by not wrapping his bag. This sort of thing can seriously impede your work and travel when there is 3 feet of snow on the ground. The opposite is true in the U.S., however, where it is advisable to keep your checked baggage unlocked—the goons from the TSA will smash their way in to check the bag's contents whatever security precautions you take.

> **Travel with a lockable suitcase that cannot be cut.**

On arrival at immigration in the destination country, march up to the desk with the shortest line—usually the diplomatic desk—and wave that same letter from your organization. This sometimes speeds up the process, sometimes not. But it's a very rare immigration official who will send you back to join the horrendous line snaking back from the "normal" desks. Much depends on how long ago the disaster occurred, and therefore the cynicism of the officer in question.

At customs in Islamic countries, make sure that you have decanted any alcohol in your checked baggage into plastic lemonade bottles before leaving home. Duty-free will be confiscated if it can be seen, but will usually be ignored if it is discreetly hidden in your carry-on bag.

On arrival in a new country with a questionable security record, arrange to be met by somebody you know, or someone carrying some pre-agreed identification (an agency logo, for example). **Let them know if your plans change or the plane is significantly delayed** as you will become deeply unpopular with the drivers, if not with your bosses, if you fail to do so. It is not just a matter of politeness.

Keep an eye on your possessions by not leaving bags unattended or open.

... taxis

The less developed the country, the less reliable the taxis. If you are not being picked up at the airport by your organization, arrange for the hotel to pick you up. If they will not, or cannot, choose another place to stay. If you are stuck, do not succumb to the entreaties of unofficial taxi drivers. Instead **use a registered airport taxi service**. Even then, **agree to the fare in advance** and have your wits about you when paying—switching a 50-dollar bill for a 20 when a tired passenger isn't looking, and then complaining that the money is not enough, is the oldest trick in the book. It happened to me in an off-guarded jet-lagged moment in Istanbul just recently.

If you are leaving a restaurant late in the evening, ride with another person going in roughly the same direction, even if this means taking a rather longer route home. **Ask the restaurant to call the taxi.** Even small places will be only too happy to give the business to someone in their (extended) family, and they know that their reputation and business—not to mention honor—will be at stake should something happen to you. Taking an open-air "tuk-tuk" in Asia is fun but ill-advised, as it leaves you open to opportunistic bag theft or worse. But I do it all the time, and nothing has ever happened to me.

It is not unknown for a taxi driver to detour down some ill-lit backstreet, having alerted some of his friends by cell phone that he has a passenger just off a plane (and therefore probably loaded with cash) ripe for robbing. The same can happen when leaving a restaurant "slightly the worse for wear." This happened to a Danish friend of mine in Bangkok recently. Luckily, being a muscular martial arts expert, he "persuaded" the attackers to back off before they could take anything. Once you suspect you might be being "detoured," you have two choices: get out abruptly or lock yourself in. Either way, slide over to **sit behind the driver** so that (s)he cannot observe what you are doing.

Find out where you are—there should be street signs or other landmarks to help orient you—then phone a friend, if you have one nearby who may be in a position to help, and explain your suspicions. The more the driver hears of this conversation, the better. If you are contemplating getting out at this stage, make sure your luggage is with you. But don't suddenly leap out of the vehicle in the middle of nowhere, as this will probably pose more dangers than those, until now, you are only imagining.

... jet lag and travel sickness

Long-haul travel affects everyone differently. To mitigate its more zombie-inducing effects, it helps to do the following:

> Drink no coffee or alcohol twenty-four hours prior to travel, but drink lots of water instead.

> Same on the plane.

> Stretch your legs and do some simple stretching exercises every two hours or so during the flight.

> Use lots of rehydrating skin cream during the flight.

> Sleep on the plane if you want/can, but adjust your sleep to the local time zone once you have landed (i.e., do not be tempted to nap during the day; just have an early night).

> At about midday local time, energy levels will be low, wherever you are. Get out into the sun, drink more water, eat fruit and resist the temptation to nap.

Travel- or motion-sickness is normally experienced in vehicles and boats. Some people swear that the use of elasticated bands that apply pressure to certain points on the underside of the wrist limit the effects of nausea. Others say that sitting on a newspaper works, too. Many are equally convinced that drugs (e.g., 10mg. of domperidone/Motilium) are the only solution. But, for me, such drugs induce a zombielike state that lasts for days, so I don't use them. In northern Pakistan, the local Pathans chew raw ginger. Judging by the vomit stains smeared down the sides of the "jingly" buses that jolt from dusty town to dusty town, this doesn't appear too effective. For most, though, sitting in the front of a vehicle and not reading anything keeps the worst at bay.

... **an air crash**

REALITY CHECK

A U.K. Army Air Corps helicopter observer who was learning to become a pilot with me was shot down during the Falklands conflict in 1982 and crash-landed into the sea. The Gazelle helicopter turned upside down and sank almost immediately. He remembers it being very dark, very cold and very quiet under the water.

Despite all his training, he could not unfasten his six-point harness. There is an emergency quick-release button, but he didn't use it. Instead, he methodically cut his way out of all six straps as the aircraft went down. He even dropped the knife (every military pilot has one of these—attached to a piece of cord—sewn into the ankle of their flying suit) and remembers hauling it back up while thinking "At least I now know which way to go to reach the surface." Both he and his pilot survived.

Surprisingly, given the media attention air crashes attract, traveling by air in a fixed-wing aircraft is the safest form of transport per mile traveled of them all (but not the safest per journey; that title goes to rail travel).

I'm not sure if the statistics hold true for the UN, however, who tend to use the cheapest old airframes still airworthy (i.e., former Soviet stock)... hurtling down a dirt-strip runway in an old Antonov with the loadmaster on his back struggling to close the door with his feet will be a scene familiar to UN logisticians working in much of the world.

People walk away from 92 percent of plane crashes.

Most people believe that if they're in a plane crash their time is up. In fact, the truth is surprising, as the survivors of the "ditching" of an American Airlines plane into the Hudson River, New York, in January 2009 will attest. In the U.S. alone, between 1983 and 2000, there were 568 plane crashes. Out of the collective 53,487 people onboard, 51,207 survived. People walk away from over 92 percent of air crashes. You will increase your chances of doing so, even in relatively small aircraft such as those used by NGOs and the UN in remote places, by considering the following and **making a mental emergency escape plan before you take off**:

> Statistically, there is no seat on any aircraft that is safer than another; your chance of survival depends on the type of crash-landing endured. You may feel more secure, however, sitting next to the emergency exit. If you do, study how to open the door before takeoff.

> The "brace position" will offer you the best chance to survive in a crash because it stops you from flying forward and striking the seat in front of you. The important thing is to get your upper torso down as far as possible, limiting the jackknife effect of impact forces. **Rest your head on the seat back in front of you with your hands folded (not clasped with fingers entwined) behind your head.** This is when "you kiss your ass good-bye," as the saying goes.

> Many plane crashes have a postcrash fire. But it's not the flames that are likely to kill you, it's the toxic smoke. Smoke onboard is thick and lethal; in just a few breaths you can pass out. And if you have to evacuate in smoke, finding the exit is very difficult. But there is one simple step you can take that could increase your

chances of escaping in the presence of smoke: **count the seat rows from you to the nearest exit** (which, as some airlines are fond of reminding you, can be behind you) so that you can feel your way to an exit by counting the rows of seats as you crawl past. And, in the event of smoke, you will need to crawl to **get your mouth as close as possible to the floor**, where the available air will be cleaner.

> Practice unbuckling your seat belt before takeoff, as the fastening method is not like the one your brain is used to using in a car. Most air-crash survivors, including the helicopter pilots in the "reality check" on page 147, report difficulties in getting out of their seats because they tried to release the straps as if they were in a car.

... air travel and disease

Commercial aircraft are equipped with environmental-control systems that monitor and control pressurization, air flow, air filtration and temperature. In an effort to conserve fuel, 50 percent or more of the air in the cabin is recycled. For the same reason, oxygen content is reduced. The recycled air passes through high-efficiency particulate air (HEPA) filters, similar to those used in hospital respiratory isolation rooms, once every three minutes or so.

Despite these systems, there is concern among travelers about the possible spread of communicable diseases during air travel. Infections of particular concern include tuberculosis, meningitis, measles, SARS and the various "swine" and "avian" influenzas. There is concern, too, among pilots—who fly every day and are therefore more exposed to possible contaminants than even their "frequent flyer" passengers—about the apparent increase in neurological disorders associated with being in the cockpit. Are these concerns justified?

From investigations of disease outbreaks associated with air travel, two main risk factors for the spread of communicable diseases have been identified: flight duration and seating proximity to the source.

Only one investigation has documented transmission of **tuberculosis** (TB) from a symptomatic passenger to six other passengers who were seated in the same section of a commercial aircraft during a long-haul flight (over eight hours), none of whom contracted active TB. The HEPA filters described above are able to filter out TB *Mycobacteria*. Nevertheless, anyone with active TB is discouraged from flying, as proximity to other passengers means that infection can occur before filtration.

Measles is a highly contagious viral disease. Since a person infected with measles is contagious from the first onset of vague symptoms (up to four days before the rash appears) to approximately four days after the development of the rash, the potential for disease transmission during air travel is a concern. Despite this, very few cases of measles have been documented as a direct result of in-flight exposure. Travelers should ensure they are immunized if they have not had the disease.

Influenza is highly contagious, particularly among people in enclosed spaces. This includes airplanes. As with TB, transmission of flu viruses is associated with proximity to source. New strains of **avian and swine (H1N1) influenza** viruses have been shown to cause infection in humans, although with, so far, limited potential for human-to-human transmission. Because influenza viruses are very adept at changing, there is concern that these strains could eventually mutate, become a threat and thus affect air travel.

SARS was first identified in southern China in November 2002 and recognized as a global threat by March 2003. It is caused by a new coronavirus. In spite of the clear role of international travel in the spread of SARS during the 2003 outbreak, only one case of in-flight transmission has been confirmed.

To reduce the international spread of mosquitoes and other insect vectors, a number of countries require disinfection of all in-bound flights. This involves spraying the aircraft cabin with an aerosol insecticide (usually 2 percent phenothrin) while passengers are onboard. Although such disinfection was declared safe by WHO in 1995, there is still much debate about the safety of the agents and methods used. Passengers have reported reactions to both the aerosols and residual insecticides, including rashes, respiratory irritation, burning eyes and tingling and numbness of the lips and fingertips. Despite such reports, there is no evidence to prove a causal relationship. To avoid ingestion of the insecticide, it might be prudent to inhale through a handkerchief for a couple of minutes after the spraying.

Deep Vein Thrombosis (DVT) occurs when blood passing through the deepest veins in the calf or thigh flows so slowly that a solid clot forms. DVTs themselves are not life-threatening, but they are associated with complications that can be fatal. For instance, a piece of the clot can break off and become lodged in the lungs, resulting in a potentially fatal pulmonary embolism.

The risk of developing DVT is thought to be increased by air travel—particularly long flights. But sitting still for long periods does not alone explain why air passengers are at higher risk of these potentially deadly blood clots. Dutch research suggests low air pressure and oxygen levels on long-haul flights play a role, although it also highlights other potential factors such as stress and air pollution.

Getting There

Driving

How to deal with ...

We all find ourselves driving an unfamiliar car on the wrong side of the road in an unfamiliar place at some time or another. This might be in a relatively benign urban environment but is just as likely to be in an "extreme" off-road situation. I have had to manhandle my car over a dried-up wadi in Morocco, build a bridge over an impassable stream in Rwanda, float the car by raft in the swamps of South Sudan and inch along precipitous mountain tracks half-eaten away by rock slides in Kashmir.

The biggest single cause of injury in the course of carrying out humanitarian work is an accident involving vehicles. Nevertheless, as in "normal" life, avoidable accidents are far too common. The wearing of a seat belt will prevent, or at least reduce, injuries sustained on the road. Wear your seat belt, not just because it might save your life but because your insurance won't pay out if you don't.

Driving in conflict zones poses additional hazards, and it is as well to know what to do when confronted by men waving guns around.

... driving alone

Do not drive alone, especially at night, and especially after social occasions. If you insist on doing so, **keep the windows closed**—or open no more than 6 inches (10 cm) if there is no air-conditioning—in built-up areas **and doors locked**.

If you are threatened or forced to pull over, reverse away sounding your horn. If ramming is necessary, hit the back of the target vehicle, as this is lighter than the front where the engine is located. At all times, **maintain enough distance between you and the vehicle in front** so that you can escape if necessary.

Sad to say, **do not be tempted to pick up hitchhikers and do not stop to help what appears to be a stranded motorist**—such people are often not what they appear to be.

Install automatic gates at home—or hire guards who can open the gates for you—so that you don't have to get out of the vehicle to open them yourself. This is when most carjackings or robberies are attempted.

... defensive driving

REALITY CHECK

Hashim, a driver working for the World Health Organization, was driving down the Fallujah road out of Baghdad in July 2003—i.e., some three months since the Iraq War had ended—in the middle vehicle of a convoy of three large white UN 4x4s. He remembers a gray Toyota pulling up alongside as they sped at nearly 60 miles per hour down the deserted highway. Slowly, as if in a dream, right next to him the tinted windows were manually wound down and two men clumsily tried to maneuver their Kalashnikov assault rifles through the gap. He remembers them struggling with the cocking levers in the confined space and the barrels wobbling in the slipstream as they aimed right at him. One of the men even knocked his magazine off onto the tarmac speeding past below. He had time to replace it with another before the firing started. Amazingly, only one man died that day—and Hashim was not even hit, despite being only a few feet away.

What is remarkable about this story is not that the gunmen took over fifteen seconds to start shooting. Nor that only one person was hit. It is that Hashim spent the entire time driving at the same speed in the same direction. He said later that he never even thought of braking or swerving into them. . . .

Personnel working in potentially hostile environments—whether at risk of robbery in Nairobi or carjacking in Albania—are at most risk when in transit from place to place. Terrorists, hostage takers and other hostile elements are well aware of this fact and are committed to exploiting it. **Defensive driving involves essential skills that prevent incidents before they occur** and ensures you respond quickly and effectively when they do. With the primary focus on prevention, a high level of awareness is demanded on your part and concentration is needed to anticipate hazards.

... **an accident**

REALITY CHECK

Driving the lead vehicle in a food-aid convoy through a village in central Bosnia in 1993, Christian's driver accidentally ran over and killed a child. Of course, they stopped, aghast at what had happened. Within seconds, a wailing mother had appeared and began hurling abuse at them both. As is the case in such situations, not much could be done to calm her down except wait for the police. But this was a war zone and there were no police.

Within minutes, a large and increasingly angry crowd had appeared, bent on exacting revenge for this dreadful accident. In the melee, Christian, who was now being dragged by the quick-thinking driver of the truck behind him into the safety of his cab, remembers hearing a shot being fired. His unfortunate driver, now lying dead in the middle of the road, was then hacked to pieces by the mob with pitchforks and scythes.

Whether you are driving or not, if there is an incident, **do not stop** the vehicle until well away and out of sight. This, unfortunately, applies even if someone has been run over. The reason for this apparently callous act is that family members will not be far away and have been known to take the law into their own hands—as the "reality check" above confirms. Instead, drive on to find a local doctor or nurse, hand over your medical kit and give him or her a lift back to near (but out of sight of) the scene of the accident. Only later report the incident to the authorities.

If you run someone over, do not stop.

... drivers

Arriving for the first time in Bujumbura, Burundi, I was met by a uniformed driver holding an EU flag. His name was Apollinaire. Barking at the porter to carry my bags, he led me to a white Mercedes parked in the VIP section. The car was brand new, complete with hood flag, chrome wheels and tinted windows. "Wow," I thought, "they really know how to look after you here." It wasn't until I struggled to open the door—which must have weighed half a ton—that I realized it was armour-plated with glass at least 1 inch thick. Having spent far too much of the previous three years being shelled and shot at in Bosnia, my immediate thought was: "I wonder why it's armored?" It didn't take long to find out.

Apollinaire wended his way around the potholes that might once have formed a road toward the Novotel where I was staying, explaining as he went that this was the EC delegate's car but since he was away, I, as his deputy, could use it. Evidently it was so new that he hadn't even used it himself. Having dropped my bags, the two of us set off again to attend the daily UN security briefing so that I could find out what was going on.

Negotiating Bujumbura traffic makes Parisian driving seem orderly. Cars would screech around the only *carrefour* in town, going clockwise or anticlockwise as the mood took them. Traffic lights—those that worked anyway—were ignored completely. Similarly, the market was a teeming tumult of garishly clad Hutu women running and shouting, babies wrapped tightly against their backs, with enormous wicker baskets of all kinds of fruit, vegetables and flowers. I had never seen such vibrant colors. Or such frenetic activity.

But I couldn't hear a thing. Armored vehicles are so protected that the windows don't wind down and microphones are needed to hear what is going on outside. So when three muffled thuds permeated the air-conditioned silence, I assumed it was someone slapping the roof with their hand. Even the sound of what appeared to be tinkling glass didn't seem out of the ordinary. It was only when women and children started running in all directions and falling over in blind panic, leaving their fruit and vegetables rolling around in the street, that I realized something must be up.

Driving

Apollinaire, who had been trying to keep a reasonable distance from the vehicle in front, smoothly swung the Mercedes past the now-stalled traffic and accelerated away across the suddenly deserted square, not stopping until we were within the UN compound gates some five minutes later. We pulled up next to an openmouthed gaggle of UN and NGO aid workers staring in disbelief. I thought this a bit strange.

I couldn't open my door for some reason, so Apollinaire let me out the other side. I could not believe what I saw when I walked around the car. The side I had been sitting on was riddled with jagged holes. The windows were pockmarked as if hit very hard with a large hammer and the tires were shredded. The three thuds I had dimly heard were, it later transpired, the noise of three hand grenades being thrown at—or at least near—the car. The tinkling sound was from the shrapnel.

I had been in the country for less than two hours and that car—its armor plating and run-flat tires—saved my life. Or, rather, Apollinaire had. For if he'd not had room to maneuver out of trouble, we might never have got away.

Most organizations insist on their international staff being driven by a locally hired driver when in the field (including capital cities). While this may appear neo-colonialist to some, the fact is that national staff can be reassigned in the aftermath of an accident, whereas international staff may have to leave the country—thereby causing massive disruption to ongoing aid programs.

Your driver is a vital resource. Apart from holding your life in his hands (I have yet to meet a she—although apparently UNICEF appointed two female drivers in Islamabad recently) while driving and negotiating checkpoints, he will be a mine of local social, political and cultural information. Listen to him.

Some drivers, however, have a tendency to show off their driving skills if they think there is an important or "international" passenger in the vehicle. This bravado is expressed by driving too fast and by taking unnecessary risks when overtaking. In my experience, this tendency increases in direct proportion to perceived status, i.e., vehicle size. **Do not be afraid to instruct the driver to slow down.** It must be made clear that this is not a suggestion, it is an instruction. If all else fails, insist you take over the driving yourself as this person is putting you in danger.

An attractive female friend of mine working with the Swiss government says it is not uncommon to receive inappropriate comments from so-called professional male drivers. Not surprisingly, this makes her uncomfortable. She recounts that what begins as overt flattery (accompanied by much use of the rearview mirror) escalates to the point that she gets taken on the "scenic route" instead of going straight to her meeting, and has even culminated in the gift of a set of underwear. She kicks herself now for being too trusting and for not "nipping the situation in the bud." This is, after all, sexual harassment and cannot be tolerated. If it continues after one "friendly" verbal warning, it must be stopped with a formal written complaint (see **hiring and firing** section).

In more male-dominated societies, it may not be appropriate for a woman to travel alone with a locally hired male driver (and the woman recounting the story above perhaps should have thought of this). If this is unavoidable, she should definitely not be seated in the front seat beside the driver but behind him. Out of respect for the dignity of all concerned, you may wish to ensure that there is a female companion or family member present, especially for longer trips in rural areas, which tend to be more conservative.

... **evading roadblocks**

REALITY CHECK

Bumping down the dirt track that winds along the northern shoreline of Lake Tanganyika, we eventually reached the border crossing between Burundi and the Congo. The frontier post, a small mud hut with a rusting tin roof, appeared to be deserted, with nothing more than a rope and a few empty plastic beer crates barring our way. There had been insurgencies in this cross-border zone for some time and nonmilitary vehicles were something of a rarity.

Out of nowhere, a small group of heavily armed soldiers converged on our vehicle, guns pointing menacingly. I was driving. As is usual in this part of the world, uniforms were anything but uniform. Some wore black wellington boots, some wore sneakers and some no footwear at all. Some wore berets and others sported baseball caps. But each was using four or five turns of pink climbing rope as a belt, with a carabiner as a buckle. And each stared impassively through what appeared to be brand-new Ray-Ban sunglasses. These were not the usual sleepy and corrupt border guards. Nor were they "ordinary" soldiers. Something was up.

The tallest of the bunch told us to get out of the car. Through the half-open window, I politely declined, saying that we were nonmilitary, neutral aid workers on our way to resupply the health clinic in Uvira, a mile or so down the road. At this apparent insubordination, the tall soldier slowly raised his AK-47 and fired a short burst of automatic fire over the roof of the car. The implication was as obvious as the noise was deafening. And a hot brass cartridge case hit me hard on the cheek to reinforce the point. At least he hadn't pointed the gun at me. In the silence that followed, he asked me again, very politely and very quietly, to step out of the car. Telling the others to remain where they were, I did so.

I passed him my EC *laissez passer* (passport) and, pushing my sunglasses back onto my head, watched warily as he flicked through each page. He was holding it upside down. He motioned me to follow him to the back of the vehicle while his colleagues kept their guns trained on the car.

He wanted to unload all the contents. Once again, I protested, saying that it was medical supplies destined for a health clinic, which—I put in for good measure—his men were highly likely to benefit from one day. Looking me up and down disdainfully, he reached in and took the vehicle's first-aid kit. "This," he said, laughing now, "is your border-crossing toll."

With this, he let us go. It could have been worse. Much worse. A few weeks later, in the south of the country, the occupants of a UN vehicle were stopped by a similar bunch of soldiers, forced to kneel beside it by the roadside and summarily executed.

Armed men, some of whom could appear very hostile, may try to stop you on the road. In some places, these are "authorized" checkpoints run by de facto local authorities. In other places, they may be manned by local gangsters to extort money or steal other valuables, including vehicles. These men may be high on drugs and/or they may be frightened. Or they may just be bored.

Checkpoints are often little more than local income-generating initiatives—much depends on whether you are in or near a conflict zone or not. Use utmost discretion. If guns are in evidence or, worse, pointed at you, you are in a dangerous situation. If other gunmen can be seen lolling under the nearest tree, the situation should still be considered dangerous.

Your aim should be to reduce the chances of a violent reaction on their part.

Coming around a corner to find yourself faced with a roadblock manned by aggressive armed men leaves you with two choices: either get out of there fast or drive on and trust to your negotiation skills (see **negotiation and resolving conflict** section). The latter is recommended.

Doing a 180° turn in a moving car is a guarantee that you will be shot at. If you do take this rash action, **all passengers should lie down**. It also helps if you have practiced the maneuver before. Finally, if you anticipate this sort of encounter, **begin your journey early in the day and avoid traveling in the late afternoon**, as this is when dangerous and/or drunk men are at their most suspicious. **It is best not to travel at night if you can possibly avoid it.**

Assuming you have taken the sensible choice, **drive slowly up to the checkpoint**—often little more than some string strung between two old beer crates—**undoing your seat belts, turning off any music and turning the radio volume right down as you approach.** Once you have stopped, **wind down your window enough to allow conversation but not wide enough to allow arms to reach in. Leave the engine running** unless told not to. If it's getting late, **turn off your headlights**, leaving the sidelights on. Nervous soldiers don't like being dazzled by headlights. **Turn on your inside light** so that those outside can see in.

> **Checkpoints are more hostile in the late afternoon.**

Make no sudden movements. Even reaching to unbuckle your seat belt may be construed as a potentially hostile act, which is why you undid it as you approached.

Whatever you do, **never start talking on the radio** in the vicinity of the roadblock, as paranoid gunmen will think you are a spy and be much more suspicious as a result.

Any accompanying armed escort should return fire only if fired upon first, and, for legal reasons, must have been briefed accordingly prior to the convoy setting off.

When asked for your papers, **maintain eye contact and hand over your identity card or passport**. If the papers are returned but you are not waved through, **tuck approximately 50 cents' worth of local currency in the last page of the document** and try again. Keep doing this until you are allowed/let through. If you are ordered out of the car, suggest that this is unwise because you are affiliated with the UN or an embassy (any embassy except those of France, the UK or the US, as these are widely perceived to be part of any local conflict) and you have diplomatic privilege.

If any single occupant is unhappy with the situation and does not want to proceed, turn back.

If you decide to turn around and the roadblock is more than 150 yards away, **stop the car fast**. **Reverse at high speed while looking at the roadblock (i.e., do not look in the rearview mirror). Change gear into neutral and swing the front wheels as fast as you can a quarter-turn to the right. As the front of the car swings around under the momentum of the engine's weight, engage second gear and drive away as fast as you can, weaving from side to side in the road if there is room.**

If you are closer than 150 yards, you are facing a "handbrake turn" scenario: **accelerate gently to 35 miles per hour, engage the clutch to disengage the gears, turn the wheel slightly left and at the same time pull on the handbrake with as much force as you can. The slight left turn will cause the now-skidding rear wheels to slide around. Engage first gear and, when the rear wheels are facing the roadblock, drive away as fast as you can.**

Again, **weave the car if you can**; it is very difficult for semitrained and probably drunk soldiers to hit a target on which they cannot properly take a bead (aim). Another one to practice before you are faced with doing it for real, especially if road conditions are wet or dusty.

If you are unlucky enough to be confronted by the type of boy soldiers seen in the film *Blood Diamond*, then you will probably be on the road in a big white car with a radio. If you have time to do so, use it to **tell base your location and the nature of your problem**. Because you do have a problem, especially if it is late in the day. But boy soldiers, drugged, drunk or intoxicated with bloodlust as they usually are, are still boys. Usually, and unlike in the film, it is possible to negotiate with them therefore, but slightly differently from the way you would with adults.

As when stopped by their older brethren, **stay in the car unless explicitly told to get out**. **Offer cigarettes** as they look at your papers (which they will probably be holding upside down), but don't be too quick to do this—it may become a useful negotiating tactic later. As soon as you can, **move the conversation to soccer**. This is a universal language and all aid workers should know at least one current and interesting fact connected with the sport—even if it's only knowing which club David Beckham now plays for. If things get tense, move soccer from conversation to action. This may even extend to **playing soccer with them**. But let them win!

Remove your sunglasses when negotiating.

Take your sunglasses off and put them on your head. Be prepared to trade them but don't give them away for nothing in return. Trading establishes dialogue. Anything sweet is appreciated more by children than men. Best of all is to **always have a few soccer "valves" in your pocket** (see **influencing people** section). These are the little (and cheap) pieces of metal that link a bicycle pump to a soccer ball, thereby enabling it to be inflated. Bicycle pumps are commonplace in developing countries (soccer balls less so), but valves are not and are worth more than their weight in gold. Ballpoint pens are also useful bargaining chips.

In summary, the following checklist should be understood by all those traveling with you when operating near conflict zones. It is always a good idea to verbally **run through this list with everybody before**

setting off, especially when there are two cars (minimum) traveling in convoy:

> Maintain at least 100 yards between vehicles at all times. So when the first vehicle reaches the checkpoint, the second stops 100 yards short.

> Turn the radio to low volume or off, to avoid it attracting attention at the checkpoint.

> Whatever else you do, do not speak on the radio in sight of those stopping you, as this makes them especially nervous.

> Observe the checkpoint from a distance, without stopping, to understand what is happening there. Does everything appear normal? Or are there signs that there may be a problem?

> If you suspect that there is a risk of violence or other serious problems, turn around and drive steadily away, if it is safe to do so.

> All passengers should remove their sunglasses before arriving at the checkpoint.

> Keep valuables out of sight. It is best to travel without valuables, if possible.

> If you are traveling at night, switch off headlights, leaving sidelights on, and switch on the interior light so that the checkpoint guards can see the vehicle occupants.

> Approach the checkpoint slowly and stop several yards before the barrier.

> Remain inside the vehicle unless you are ordered to get out.

> Make no sudden movements. Even moving your hand to release the seat belt could sometimes be interpreted as reaching for a weapon—so announce what you are doing before you do it and move slowly.

> If one person is asked to come away from the vehicle, for example to an office to check papers, consider whether it is safer for another person to accompany him/her.

> Be ready to answer questions about the occupants, your journey, the vehicle and anything in it.

> One person should be nominated to do the talking, on behalf of all the occupants, unless questions are put directly to other occupants.

**Make no sudden movements.
Do not speak on the radio.**

> Be ready to show any relevant documents, including vehicle documents, authorizations, copies of passports and ID cards. If possible, avoid showing the original of your passport, to avoid it being stolen—but in some cases the original may be required. Keep your ID card on a cord around your neck so that you can show it without surrendering it.

> If you suspect that the checkpoint may have a hostile intention, depending on the circumstances it may be sensible to keep all doors, including the cargo door, locked, with windows more than halfway up. But in some circumstances this may anger soldiers or police, so use your judgment as to which is best.

> Allow the car to be searched if they insist on it. If you are traveling in a clearly marked UN or Red Cross vehicle, politely point out that these organizations are not NGOs but impartial and neutral global organizations before acquiescing.

> If threatened with a weapon, comply calmly with instructions.

> Have a clear policy on giving lifts. Humanitarian staff are often asked to give lifts to soldiers at checkpoints, armed or unarmed. Most humanitarian organizations forbid giving lifts to any military personnel.

> If any single occupant is unhappy with the situation and does not want to proceed, turn back.

... **carjacking**

Returning home one night in Albania's capital, Tirana, in 1999, I found myself confronted by two balaclava-wearing, gun-toting bandits. As I stepped down slowly and carefully from my vehicle, it quickly became apparent that it was the car they wanted and not me. "Phew, at least it's not a kidnapping attempt," I thought. While one gestured for me to stand by the wall with his gun barrel, the other climbed into the vehicle. A shouting match between the two of them then ensued in Albanian.

After a few minutes of this, the one in the car got out and made me get back in. The problem became clear: this being a British car (a Land Rover Discovery), the steering wheel was on the "wrong" side of the car. It was also not automatic and neither of them knew what a clutch was. So I then had to teach them how to get the car into reverse. While this went on, they calmed down noticeably, to the extent that all three of us actually began to laugh.

In this spirit, I asked if I could remove my wallet and house keys, which were in the glove compartment. They agreed. But, for some obscure reason, they would not let me keep Noel Malcolm's newly published book on Kosovo, which was lying on the backseat. Strange.

After firing a few shots in the air (to regain their bravado, I assume), they eventually drove off. The car was found abandoned a few days later, having run out of fuel. The key to the lockable filler cap was with my house keys!

Passengers are most vulnerable to kidnap attempts while in a vehicle. Potential hostage takers know this. Most often, carjack attempts take place as you slow to enter the family home—as indeed was the case in the "reality check" above. To minimize this risk, either **call your guards to say you are approaching**, so that they can open the gate, or install automatic gates. It is better still to have more than one entrance/exit and use them randomly.

Carjack attempts on the road are most likely to be made in one or more vehicles. One will swoop in front of you and block your forward progress. Another will attempt to block you from the side or from behind. The challenge is knowing the difference between a genuine kidnap attempt and just plain bad driving. **In a kidnap attempt, the**

car in front will stop almost perpendicular to your direction of travel and disgorge armed men.

As a defensive driver, you will have been doing your utmost to **maintain enough distance between you and the vehicle in front** so that you can swerve around any attempt to block your path.

Once you realize the situation you are in, aim to crash into the center of the blocking vehicle's rear wheel with one of your bumper mounts (the mounts are usually located about a foot closer to the center of your car than the tire.) Not only does this minimize damage to your vehicle but more important it transmits the maximum force to the blocking vehicle. **A properly placed blow at 15 mph will easily spin your opponent clear.**

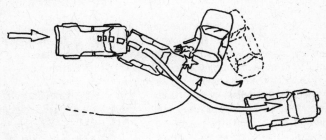

Approach the blocking vehicle relatively slowly, then accelerate hard in the last few yards to punch it out of the way. A lower speed reduces the chance of damaging your vehicle: you're in trouble if you bend your suspension or steering and wind up motionless 200 yards away from the ambush site.

If gunmen are in the way, too bad for them. Keep going. The jolt as you hit is noticeable but not enough to cause injury to your passengers, who should now be ducking down since bullets are likely to be coming your way.

In the event that a car with clearly hostile intent draws up alongside, draw imperceptibly away and then suddenly and without warning reverse direction and ram your vehicle as hard as you can into the other. Unlike what you see in the movies, the energy imparted by such a sideways hit will send the opposing car off the road. Your car will bounce back, so be prepared to correct the steering when this happens. As soon as you have made contact, hit the brakes as hard as you can. As you screech to a halt, consider whether to go on or turn around. Either way, drive to the nearest place where people will be around 24/7. This could be a police, fire or gas station.

If you are held up at gunpoint:

> Do not resist
> Cooperate and do not offend
> Make no rapid movements
> Offer the keys
> Negotiate terms
  (e.g., water, footwear, radio)

If you are forced from your vehicle at gunpoint, the chances are they want to rob you, not kill or kidnap you. Indulge them. **Smile and make sure any eye contact is neither nervous nor aggressive.** Make sure you **remove any dark glasses** so that your eyes can be seen, remembering to **keep movements slow** and **keeping the palms of your hands facing the man closest to you.** This demonstrates submissiveness and shows you are not armed and pose no threat. **Offer them the car keys** (which should still be in the car because you have left the engine running in case a quick getaway is possible). If they want more, offer them whatever other money and valuables you have before being asked. **Do not try to conceal money.** If they find money that you have not "declared," things are likely to turn nasty. Your aim is to stay alive, not rich.

> It is not worth risking your life for possessions that are either not yours or that you can easily replace.

... bogged vehicles

Unsticking vehicles from mud holes, sand dunes and snowdrifts is something you will have to get good at. There is one right way to do this and lots of wrong ways, which will leave you exhausted and the vehicle still stuck. Take time to prepare and discuss which way the unsticking team will adopt. Make sure the correct winching equipment is available before setting off. I have lost count of how many times I have had to help extricate a vehicle...

If you get stuck, first ascertain why and on what you are stuck, as you often have to jack yourself up at the same time as pulling yourself out. If one or more wheels is stuck in a hole, for example, the vehicle will need to be lifted so that the hole can be filled in before recovery is attempted.

Usually, coming out **backward is best**, as gear ratios are lower and the firmness of the ground known. **Reduce vehicle weight** first, especially if it is a loaded truck that is stuck. **Engage four-wheel drive** (if it's not already a permanent feature) **and differential ("diff") lock**, remembering to disengage both when freed. The differential allows wheels on the same axle to turn at different speeds—as when going around a corner, for example. Engaging the lock stops all the engine power being transferred to the wheel that is easiest to spin. (Note that older vehicles may have knobs on the wheel hubs that need to be turned to engage the diff lock.)

> **Remember to disengage the "diff" lock when free.**

Begin by "rocking" the car using alternate rapid reverse and first-gear changes and then, as the back wheels of the vehicle reach the highest point of the rocking cycle, **reverse the vehicle out using all the power available**. It helps to be towed or winched at one end, with people pushing at the other.

Before deciding whether the winch is needed or not, **dig the sand/ mud/snow out from under the wheels** in whichever direction you are trying to drag the vehicle out. **Put down sand-ladders**, if you have them, as near to the wheels as you can get them. Use sacks, bits of wood or any other load-spreading material if you don't, but remember they will come flying out once the revolving wheel bites. **Reducing tire pressure by half** (i.e., until the tires just begin to visibly deflate) helps spread the load and increases traction in soft going (but you will need a pump to reinflate). This is also very effective in snow, when you can let out almost all the air for increased grip.

You've tried all of the above and you're still stuck. The first thing you'll need to do is find a suitable anchor point for winching. This can be a large rock, a tree or a buried spare wheel (to the depth of a few feet). As you might imagine, the anchor point is critical to the success of the winching. If your anchor point won't hold, you'll never get your vehicle unstuck. If you are using a tree (or a number of small trees tied together), use the lowest part of the trunk as the anchor point.

Once you've picked a suitable anchor spot, disengage the clutch of the winch. On many winches, this is done by twisting a knob on one end of the unit. When the clutch has been disengaged, take the hook and begin to pull the cable out to your anchor point. The cable should unspool easily from the drum as you are pulling.

You'll need to wrap nylon webbing straps around your anchor point. **Do not wrap the winch cable around your anchor and attach the hook back on to the cable itself.** This can dangerously fray the cable and cause it to break under tension. Instead, attach the winch hook to the shackle that is fastening the straps around the anchor point. Re-engage the clutch on the winch to take it out of free-spool mode.

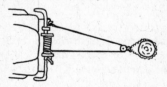

Keep as straight a line as possible from the winch to your anchor point. Also, don't try to use the winch as a hoist. It's not designed for that and you invite injury to yourself and damage to the winch and cable. **Don't winch if there are less than five wraps of cable around the drum.**

When attempting to winch out another vehicle with your own, anchor your vehicle to another vehicle or any other fixed object using your tow rope. **Attach it to your vehicle at the same end as your winch**; otherwise you risk stretching your vehicle's frame.

If there is no winch but there is a cable or rope available, it is possible to wrap it around one of the drive wheels and use the rotating wheel as an improvised winch. Reduce the air pressure in the tire slightly and use the lowest gear possible.

Even when new, cable strands can produce small, sharp protrusions of individual wire. These little wires can slice right into your hands as you're playing out the cable, so **wear tough leather gloves**.

The most common winch accident is getting your fingers caught in the cable as the last of it winds onto the drum. **Always use the remote control cable when winching, and keep everyone out of range of the cable**.

Be aware that a broken winch cable can have enough force in its whiplash to cut through a truck's roof and windshield. Imagine what would happen if the cable met a person. A snapping cable that hits a small tree will tear the tree down. A cable that hits a large tree can wrap tightly around it, so

Drape a jacket over the cable when winching.

anyone standing behind it is not necessarily protected. Furthermore, if a cable breaks, the vehicle being winched may roll downhill, so never stand lower down a hill than any vehicle being winched. It is a good idea to **drape a heavy cloth jacket or tree branch over the cable** to limit the whiplash if something snaps.

All aid vehicles should carry a Hi-Lift Jack for lifting the vehicle and a board with a bolt through it, so the base of the jack doesn't sink into the ground and the jack does not slide off the board when it tilts (which it invariably does). The spare wheel can also be used as the base, although it is heavy and difficult to maneuver. The jack can also be used horizontally as a hand winch.

Snatch straps have revolutionized 4x4 recovery. The strap is attached to the towing point on the bogged vehicle and similarly on the recovery vehicle with a large S-shaped loop of slack in between. The recovery vehicle accelerates away, usually in first or second gear. As the strap becomes taut, it stretches, transferring kinetic energy from the recovery vehicle to the bogged vehicle, popping it free. **All bogged vehicles should generally have all four wheels rotating to assist. Spinning the wheels does not help, though. Generate maximum traction by using the lowest possible gear.** If it doesn't work, do it again, this time with more speed. Often, it will be necessary to tie two straps together. If you need to do this, make sure to **put a piece of**

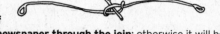

wood or a rolled-up newspaper through the join; otherwise it will be impossible to untie them later.

It is relatively easy to right an overturned car. Place a recovery vehicle with a winch at right angles to the overturned vehicle. Cut a notch in a 4-foot-long and 4x4-inch piece of hard wood and stick the other end under the chassis on the side nearest the recovery vehicle. Hold it at 45 degrees and loop the winch cable over the notch. Take the strain and stand well back. The car will turn on its side, after which a good shove from a few strong people will put it back on its wheels.

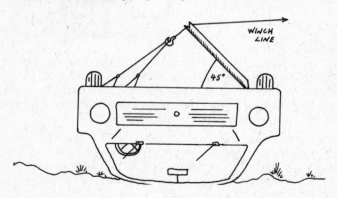

WINCH LINE

45°

... minefields

There are over 600 different types of land mines. Broadly speaking, they fall into one of two categories: anti-tank (AT) and anti-personnel (AP). Most types detonate under pressure, by tilting or by trip-wire. If you see an AT mine, the surrounding area will probably also contain AP mines.

A common type of AP mine, especially in Afghanistan, is the "butterfly" mine. Usually brightly colored to attract children, these mines are air-delivered. If one is found, it means there will be up to 2,000 more nearby. Do not be tempted to pick one up. Unless you are a mine-disposal expert, **never touch a mine.**

If you are entering an area that is likely to have been mined, ask locals what the markers for known minefields look like. Such markers might be sticks, bits of metal, painted rocks or just heaps of stones, all of which might be "invisible" to you while driving or walking past in blissful ignorance.

Never touch a mine.

Driving

173

Otherwise, you will only know you are in a minefield when you actually see a mine, or when one explodes. In both cases, everyone around you will panic. Some will go into shock, especially if there is an injury, and will need to be calmed and/or restrained. The immediate priority is to **stop all movement**, as you may already be well inside the field. Your best chance of survival is to **use the radio and wait to be rescued**. Standing still for an uncomfortably long time is better than blowing yourself up. If you absolutely must move, retrace your steps or vehicle tracks as precisely as possible. Only one person should move at a time while maintaining 25 yards between people at all times.

The reason you stopped may well be that the vehicle in front just exploded. In this case, there will be injured people, and you have to make a judgment about the level of help you can give. If there is a victim still alive, you must **resist the instinct to rush to his or her aid**, as you will most probably serve only to increase the body count. The desire to help an injured colleague is extremely powerful. But approaching a mine victim is one of the highest-risk activities known to man, so you should not feel morally obliged to do so. If the victim is communicating, reassure him or her that help is on the way and advise that further movement is not a good idea.

Think twice before attempting to aid a mine-blast victim.

If you do decide to help, **grab the trauma kit and leave your vehicle by climbing out of the window and over the front of the vehicle. Walk slowly, softly and carefully along the tracks made by the other vehicle**, and remember that some types of anti-armor mines need multiple "trips" before exploding. It may be some consolation to know that older anti-armor mines cannot be triggered by the weight of a single human walking gently. If the vehicle in front took a different route, walk back along the tire tracks made by your vehicle until the tracks made by the blown-up car coincide.

Do not try to turn the vehicle around and do not get out of the vehicle. In an area likely to be mined—in the vicinity of current or old front lines—**keep to paved roads and do not be tempted to use the shoulders**, even when turning the vehicle around. **Do not wander off to relieve yourself** either but squat by the side of the car.

Be aware that a "medevac" (medical evacuation) helicopter will not land in a known minefield. Be aware, too, that the downwash from a large helicopter such as a Chinook trying to winch you out can set off mines—as British soldiers found out to their cost in Afghanistan in 2008.

If anti-tank mines have been laid on top of the road, they are not intended to kill you; they are just a warning not to proceed farther. In such cases, you will be under observation—probably down a rifle's telescopic sight. If those watching you are

In former conflict zones, stay on the road.

prepared to let you through, they will come to you to check out who you are. If they have not done so after ten minutes or so, the message is clear, so turn around (on the road only) and try another route. Do not—as I once did in Bosnia—move the mines to one side, as they may have been booby-trapped. If the mine has antennae sticking out, do not touch—tilting that mine will not only set it off but will also trigger others nearby.

Some other safety tips to bear in mind when you are traveling in areas you suspect may have been mined:

> Don't drive over objects in the road.

> When traveling in convoy, maintain 100 yards between vehicles.

> When starting out, allow sufficient time for local traffic to have used the roads before you.

> Don't start out so late, though, that you may be forced to travel in the dark. Daylight is needed for would-be rescuers to assess the situation should you get into difficulty, and you can't read warning signs or spot clues at night.

> Be extra vigilant when driving after heavy rains, as mines, which are often encased in waterproof plastic, float and can therefore be moved by floodwater—ask anyone who has worked in Mozambique or Angola.

> If you have access to a flak jacket, sit on it in the vehicle. Wear the helmet, too, as many people are injured when their head hits the roof of the vehicle.

> When traveling on foot, allow a local guide to lead the way and maintain at least 25 yards between members of the group.

> Always carry a radio, and ensure the person carrying it (a) knows how to use it, (b) knows where you are and (c) walks near the back of the group.

Driving

175

> Never walk through overgrown areas, even if livestock are grazing nearby.

> Do not move obstacles—they may have been booby-trapped.

> Do not enter abandoned buildings.

> Talk to the population and observe behavior to find out about which areas local communities think are safe.

> Do not touch ordnance, and resist the temptation to collect war souvenirs, as many still contain explosives.

... a sinking vehicle

If you have inadvertently plunged into a river or lake, you will have a few moments to think about what to do while the air is forced out of the vehicle by the incoming water. Don't bother. **Get out of the vehicle as soon as you can. Open the door if possible** (it is possible soon after entering the water but becomes more and more difficult as the water level rises higher outside than inside). **If not, then open the windows. Break the windows if they will not wind down.** If there is nothing heavy at hand in the vehicle with which to do this, you will have to kick them out. Of all the windows, the rear window is the most difficult to reach but the weakest. Since the heavy engine is (usually) at the front, the rear will be the last part to submerge. **If there is a sunroof, exit through it as soon as you can.**

> **Escape a sinking vehicle through side windows, sunroof or kicked-out rear window.**

It is a myth that you should wait for the car to fill with water so that the doors can be opened more easily once the pressure has equalized inside and out. This does indeed happen, but only when the car has stopped sinking, i.e., it is lying on the bottom. It is extremely unlikely that you can hold your breath that long, even in a relatively shallow body of water. If you are in a fast-flowing river, the car will have begun tumbling, too, which will disorient you to the extent that you will no longer know which way is up and which way is down.

... starting the car without keys

First you have to get in. Then you have to start the engine. And then you may well have to disengage the alarm and steering lock.

Toyota Land Cruisers, Hilux pickups and Land Rovers appear to be the vehicles of choice of the international aid and business communities. They are used around the world's conflict and disaster zones because they are rugged and simple. Unless they are the newest variants, this simplicity extends to the door-locking mechanisms, which use push-button "top locks." These are locks that come straight out of the top of the inside of the car door and have levered rods set vertically inside the door itself. If you are accidentally locked out, the first thing to **try is a key from a similar make of vehicle**, as the door locks, unlike the starter lock, have some common tumblers.

If this fails, **bend a wire coat hanger into a long J** with the hook as the tail. **Square off the bottom of the J. Slide the hanger into the car door between the window and the weather strip. Feel for the end of the button rod—this will take trial and error—and lift it up.** It's that simple. As a last resort, you can always smash the side window.

There are two ways to "hot-wire" a car. The easiest involves opening the engine cover. Locate the red coil wire. **Run a wire from the positive (+) terminal of the battery to the positive side of the coil**, or the red wire that goes to the coil. Only after you have done this do you locate the starter solenoid—it is attached to the other end of the positive battery cable. **Short-circuit the two bolts on the starter solenoid using a screwdriver** and the engine will crank into life.

The harder way involves crossing (shorting) the wires bundled underneath the steering column. Each car has a different wiring loom, so this will have to be done by guesswork. Start with any red-colored wire first.

Before you are able to drive away, it may be necessary to unlock the steering wheel. **Insert a large, flat-blade screwdriver between the wheel and the steering column and push the locking pin away from the wheel by hitting it hard with a hammer.**

Driving

Most vehicles used in aid operations are older models and don't have car alarms fitted as standard. If they do, however, and the alarm has been set off, just open the engine cover and wrench the wires out of the black box making all the noise.

... off-road driving

Driving off-road over difficult terrain is exhausting. It takes a lot of focus and requires calm thought and practiced action. If you have an official driver, make sure he gets enough rest. If not, share the driving. The more difficult types of terrain call for the driver to get out and make a serious risk assessment of the possible routes.

There are three basic rules of off-road driving, especially in snow or sand:

> **Don't change gear when encountering an unexpectedly difficult spot.**
> **Use the engine for braking.**
> **Go as slowly as possible but as fast as necessary.**

The terrain will try to drive your vehicle for you. Feeling the steering wheel get pulled away from you can have dangerous repercussions. The normal reaction is to go with that feeling. Resist that urge. You must **hold the steering wheel true to course**—unless one wheel is stuck in a deep rut, in which case you don't have much choice.

Keep your thumbs outside the steering wheel.

When careering down a steep slope in a vehicle that seems like it is going to roll over, resist the urge to turn. Instead, **keep the vehicle aimed down the "fall line"** (the line a rock rolling downhill

Increase traction by reducing tire pressure.

under gravity would take). This is especially important when coming off an adverse-camber turn. Use small-input steering, holding the wheel, and don't let the terrain steer you. Make sure your thumbs are not inside the steering wheel as it can be wrenched out of your hands, which will break your thumbs.

When faced with a steep slope to go up, pick your line, hit the throttle and hold on. Discuss your line with others before you start. Be sensible. **Approach the slope slowly and let the tires bite by keeping revs high but gear low.** Try not to overspin the wheels. Stay with the line you have chosen. The vehicle will bounce around a little. Be calm and sit well back in the seat (don't lean forward, it doesn't help). Use the throttle and steering gently, and keep the revs high until well over the lip. If four-wheel drive and low-ratio gears are optional, don't forget to engage them.

In soft sand, rotating tires drag sand from the front to the rear of the tire. If you stop, even for a second, the wheel tends to dig itself into a hole as a result. To prevent this, continually steer from side to side so that the wheels steer out of their own ruts.

In deep mud, better traction will be obtained by avoiding ruts— although you can't always see these.

... fording rivers

When fording a swollen river, **choose your line by focusing on the point where the track exits on the opposite bank.** The river will be low for most of the year and there will be a more solid and more or less direct track between the entry point and the exit point. **Ask the locals,** who by now will have gathered around to watch, as sometimes there is an obvious bend in the middle. Be careful because the riverbed may be very soft on either side of this relatively hard (even though it's underwater) surface.

If the water is flowing so fast that you would not dare wade across yourself, then don't attempt to cross with the vehicle—a car quickly becomes a boat as soon as the water level is higher than halfway up the doors and it loses traction very quickly when the body lifts in the water.

> **If the river is too deep to wade across, it is too deep to drive across.**

If you do test the depth and current by trying to wade across, take a stout pole and use it as a third leg. Plant it upstream of yourself to deflect any debris.

When fording, use second gear, high revs and do not stop.

Again, if four-wheel drive and low-ratio gears are available, engage them. **Enter the water slowly but with determination.** You are trying to avoid creating a large bow wave. **Increase revs once all four wheels are in, then keep revs high and gears low** until all four wheels are safely out of the water on the far side. **Second gear is ideal. Do not be tempted to change gear and do not stop.** Many drivers stop on the far bank before the vehicle is safely on firm ground—probably out of relief—with the result that they get bogged or, worse, slip slowly backward into the torrent.

Be prepared to steer slightly upstream to counter the effects of any current. Don't worry when the water comes over the engine cover; that is why the "snorkel" air tube is attached. If there isn't one, be aware that the engine will stall as soon as water enters the air intake (i.e., when it reaches the top of the engine) or short-circuits the electrics, whichever comes first. In very deep water, **fix a tarpaulin across the radiator grille** before setting off. This will stop the force of the water pushing the fan into the radiator and, if you keep going, lower the level of water flowing around the engine block. Since the tarpaulin will also act as an enormous brake, considerably more power will be needed.

Send the first car with only a driver. Unload it first, as you don't want all your mission-critical stuff floating off downriver. **Wind down the front windows before entering the water and don't wear a seat belt** because a quick exit might be called for.

... quick-fix car repairs

If the **engine has overheated**, do not remove the radiator cap until ten minutes have elapsed, to allow the boiling water to cool. You can then remove the thermostat—not a wise move long-term, but it will get you home. If the problem is a leaky hose, duct tape will hold for weeks.

Leaking radiators can be temporarily sealed with a couple of eggs. Just put them in raw with the engine running, having refilled the radiator after giving it time to cool. Some people use ground peppercorns instead of eggs. Don't do both at the same time!

For a **squeaky fan belt**, hold a bar of soap to the outside edges of the belt while it's turning (but try not to put your hand in the fan).

When the **"charging" light** comes on, it means the alternator is not generating power. Probably this is because a belt has broken. This can be rectified by using twisted women's tights to replace the belt. Tie them with as much tension as you can.

If the **starter motor just clicks** when the key is turned, it may have developed a flat spot. Tap it sharply with a hammer to free up the brushes inside. Manually rocking the vehicle while in gear may just jiggle the brushes enough to get it started too.

Returning to the car at night only to find that the **headlights** have been left on puts a bit of a damper on the evening. Don't despair. Don't try to start the car immediately. Turn off the lights and wait fifteen minutes, as the battery may just recuperate enough in this time to turn the engine over.

If the **windshield gets a crack** in it, fill it with superglue; it won't shatter the next time a stone flies up from a passing truck. If you can't get hold of superglue, drilling a small hole all the way through the windshield at the end of the visible crack will stop it spreading further.

Dirty spark plugs that aren't firing correctly are fairly easily cleaned with oven cleaner. Soak the spark-plug tips in the oven cleaner for two hours. Scrape away leftover grime with a nail file or sandpaper.

Rusted nuts can be loosened with a thorough dousing in cola.

Driving

Smaller **dents in the bodywork** can be pulled back to more or less their original form by placing a toilet plunger over the dent, pushing down so that a vacuum is created in the rubber cup, and pulling out.

Jump leads are colored red and black for a reason; it doesn't matter which color you choose as long as you attach the negative electrode to the other negative electrode. Sometimes, the electrodes can be so dirty or oil-covered that a good connection cannot be made. Clean them with cola or something similar. Inadvertent crossing of the wires will not only cause dangerous sparking but will probably also damage the cells in the battery and blow some fuses.

Chapter 7

Managing

How to deal with ...

This section is for those who have to lead and manage teams and interface with others in field situations. It details all those intangible things that somehow you are just supposed to know about but nobody actually ever told you how to do.

... field etiquette

Use water sparingly. Two minutes in a "bucket shower" is enough, and this includes hair washing. Brushing teeth needs no more than two mouthfuls of bottled water. Be aware, however, that some people feel that brushing teeth in local tap water exposes you to local pathogens that bottled water does not and that resistance to minor diarrheal diseases is increased thereby.

It is important to **wash hands regularly** when visiting or working in health facilities or refugee camps. Experienced aid workers usually keep dry-wash or baby wipes in their pockets for this purpose.

> **It is possible to wash, shave and clean your teeth using one cup of water.**

If you are staying in an aid agency's guesthouse, **do not take food out of the fridge and eat it without the owner's permission**. You don't know what trouble might have been taken to get it there in the first place, and that last piece of moldy cheese just might be from old Aunty Nellie, providing someone in the house with an emotional link to home.

Refer to senior diplomats and ministers of state as "Your Excellency" until they ask you to call them something else. It is a good idea to use this term with rebel leaders (but only the leaders), too, however much it might stick in your throat. At least call them "Mister." You can call known heads of diplomatic missions "Ambassador," but you do not have to do this for UN staff (unless they are representing the Secretary-General), who, although having certain "diplomatic privileges," are international civil servants.

When presented to a president, call him or her "Mr. [or Madam] President." This applies whether or not the president in question is also an army general—as used to be the case in Pakistan, for example. In such cases, use military rank when in uniform (see later section on **the military**). Prime ministers are referred to as "Mr. [or Mrs.] Prime Minister."

Those with medical qualifications like to be referred to as "Dr." although it is not obligatory to do so.

When writing, start the letter simply with "Dear Sir" or "Dear Madam." End such letters with "Yours faithfully."

It is always wise to be polite to civil servants, even relatively junior ones, if you want some rapid action from them. Just drop "sir" or "madam" into the conversation from time to time.

Western women attract unwelcome "advances" from local men. The best way to rebuff such approaches without causing offense is to say: "How very kind of you, but I have to tell you that I am married and I'm not sure my husband would approve [it doesn't matter what ring is on what finger—different cultures use different fingers], and I really wouldn't want to waste your time." If they persist to the point of nuisance, plead that you have an urgent appointment. And if all else fails, tell them to call you, but give them a false phone number.

In Islamic cultures, it is a good (and respectful) idea for both men and women to cover their arms and legs at all times. For women, heads and backsides should be covered, too, when out in public.

Avoid argument and overt displays of affection in public places, as these are offensive in many cultures. Be especially sensitive to the implications of forming a relationship with locals, especially local women. In Albania, even holding the hand of a local man or woman in public is to imply an intent to "marry" and would have major repercussions for reputation, family, safety and even survival if this code (the "Kanun of Lekë Dukagjini') is not respected.

Recognize that it is not always acceptable for women to work or travel with men unless under the direct supervision of a family member. This remains the case in Iraq, for example. In such situations, consider having men travel in separate vehicles. In remoter areas of Pakistan, hiring a female necessitates that a male relative is also hired to act as "guardian."

> **If you are being pestered, give a false phone number.**

Do not point the soles of your feet at any Arab host, as this is a grave insult—just ask the Iraqi "clogger" who threw his shoes at George Bush in December 2008, only to become a national hero.

In many cultures, including Muslim ones, picking up food, accepting gifts or shaking hands with the left hand is considered an insult, as the left hand is "unclean." This also includes passing business cards, which, as for the Japanese, is more "respectfully" done using both hands.

Cameras and tape recorders quickly arouse suspicion, especially at checkpoints or near borders.

REALITY CHECK

During the 2008 South Ossetia crisis in Georgia, a Danish diplomat who was sitting next to me suddenly got out at the Russian military checkpoint outside the occupied town of Gori (Stalin's birthplace) and started taking photographs. Without hesitation, the nearest Russian soldier cocked his AK-47 and pointed it at the foolish diplomat, whose camera was confiscated never to be seen again. Having previously advised him not to leave the car, I could only shrug at his stupidity; he had put us all in harm's way—and potentially compromised the access negotiation then going on at the barrier.

Photographing military bases or strategic sites such as bridges, airstrips, border or security posts, nuclear or other similar installations is asking to have your film removed, or your camera smashed or confiscated. Even landscape backdrops can help intelligence officers pinpoint locations, so be very careful what you photograph if you don't want to be accused of spying.

In some cultures, photographing women can also get you into trouble. so **always ask permission before taking photographs**.

When negotiating with a warlord or tribal or religious leader, be aware that the order in which men enter a room, sit, greet, wash, eat and drink defines status and therefore their opinion of you. As the most senior man present—at least in the eyes of those around him, a warlord will enter the negotiating chamber (or shaded area under a tree) first. He will sit farthest from the door (or nearest the tree trunk), have his hands washed by others and eat first.

If you are already present when the warlord or leader arrives, **stand to greet him and do not sit down until he does. Sit wherever he indicates. Never start discussions without lengthy inquiries about his family, relations and general well-being, being careful not to make any specific reference to women to whom he may be related.** This can take more than half an hour. If you are negotiating in central or eastern Europe, **make sure you have eaten curds or yogurt at breakfast**—copious amounts of alcohol are likely to be consumed before mid-morning and this will prevent you from getting "tired and emotional" (i.e., inebriated) too soon.

> **Stand to greet a warlord and do not sit down until he does.**

... staying in touch

To keep in touch with loved ones far away when on limited means, consider the following:

Callback services: The provider gives you a unique number in their country, which you call for one ringtone. You hang up before it connects and there is no charge at this point. Then the payphone you called from will ring and, when you answer, you will hear a dial tone from a phone switch wherever the provider is, usually the U.S. You then dial the international number that you want to call. Callback services are actually being banned in some countries because they effectively prevent the local carriers from making money from international calls.

Internet cafés: If you are not carrying a cell phone, this is the most convenient and cheapest way to make international calls from another country. Many cafés supply headsets now, which are connected to computers running VOIP (Voice Over Internet Protocol) applications such as Skype or Yahoo. The cost per minute is cheap, even after paying for your internet access (usually around 0.02 U.S. cents per minute).

On the downside, Internet cafés offer very little privacy for your conversation and sometimes the headsets are broken or substandard. The speed of the Internet circuit and the number of users in the café will affect the quality of your call. For this reason, try to choose Internet cafés that do not look busy, or go at off-peak times when you can get a call through more easily. When you finish your call, **be sure to log off**—others could come and use your account after you leave if you don't.

You can set up a Skype account for free, and call other Skype users for free. If you want to call landlines or cell phones, you need to fund an account with at least US$10 to get started. Fortunately, the calls are so cheap that this lasts for quite a while. Sometimes calls to cell phones in certain countries can be as high as 0.4 U.S. cents per minute. And be aware when using "pay as you go" that data-streaming via Skype can exceed your limit very quickly.

Cell phones: You can use your phone in new countries by paying the international roaming rate of between US$1 and US$3 per minute. You must contact your cell phone service provider to activate international roaming before you leave. The good news is that people at home do not have to pay long-distance charges to call your phone; it still appears as a local call.

If you do not wish to pay international roaming charges— the smart choice—you can opt to **buy a prepaid SIM card** instead.

> **Use a local cell phone number and divert your international number to it.**

The SIM card is a small chip that goes inside your cell phone, usually under the battery, and it provides you with a local number in the country you are visiting. The card will come with some minutes, but you can add minutes online or at kiosks in different places. Calls made locally will be around 0.05–0.25 U.S. cents and calls made back to Europe or the U.S. will be up to 0.5 U.S. cents a minute. The bad news is that anyone calling you from home now has to pay international long-distance charges because your number is no longer local. You can switch your phone back to your old number simply by removing the SIM card. To get started using a SIM card, you may have to have your cell phone hardware "unlocked," which means taking it to a local provider or a shop where they can enter a code to allow your number on their network. Some shops do this for free while others charge for the service.

If you have left your phone charger behind, pop into the nearest large hotel and ask whether they have one you can borrow. Hotels have large collections of these—you are not the only one to have forgotten the charger. The chances of them having one that is compatible with your phone is so high that they will probably have more than one—in which case they may let you have one for free.

> **Larger hotels have a stock of left-behind phone chargers that you can borrow.**

Laptops: In former Soviet countries, linking your laptop's modem to the phone line requires that the cable be spliced onto the telephone cable. You will need a pocketknife and electrical (or "insulating") tape for this as it involves taping together exposed wires—there are two wires; it doesn't matter which is spliced with which. Make sure the splice is done under the carpet as house/hotel owners tend to take a dim view of this practice. But, because the cables are incompatible, there are no other options if you want to establish a dial-up connection.

Most NGO employers engaging in humanitarian work in remote places allow at least one free call home per week depending on satellite connectivity. They do this because they understand the contribution such calls make to a volunteer's morale and hence continued work output.

Bandwidth limitations are a major constraint to communications when working long hours in deep-field situations for everyone. When using small portable units such as R-BGAN, one photograph can take twenty minutes or more to upload.

... **media interviews**

You are being interviewed because you are considered to be knowledgeable in your field. It follows therefore that you must know your facts and be aware of any recent changes that may have occurred within your subject or situation. If you don't, **or if you have not recently been in the affected area**, then **don't do the interview**.

Before the interview, make sure you have found out:

> **what the interview is going to be about**

> **what angle the journalist will take**

> **who else the journalist is talking to**

> **whether it will be live** or prerecorded for later broadcast

Have three points you want to make; whatever the question, make these three points. **Do enough homework to be able to justify these**

three points and tell the interviewer beforehand that you intend to make them. Remove all extraneous and unwanted material so you are left with a headline sentence or "sound bite" for each message. A sound bite is a quotable statement: brief, self-contained, phrased in everyday language and roughly three seconds long, it should be clear, concise and punchy.

> **Look at the interviewer not the camera when talking on TV.**

It is always sensible to have **prepared answers to the most difficult questions**. Write these down and discuss them with colleagues or bosses prior to the interview. One of them is bound to be along the lines of "Why were you so slow to respond?" **Ask the interviewer what questions he or she intends to ask** (professionals from national networks will not ask "trick" questions). If you are asked an overtly political question, duck it and reiterate one of the three points you wanted to make.

There is no need to rehearse; just talk slowly and clearly.

As with any form of public speaking, **take ten slow, deep breaths before you go on** (you can do this in full view of others and without appearing to have just run a marathon), and **take a drink of water immediately prior to speaking**. Watch carefully and you will see seasoned politicians doing this before delivering a speech. Chewing gum helps, too, as it stops the mouth from drying. But get rid of it before speaking.

In the field, a TV interviewer will stand beside or behind the camera. Someone will ask for quiet and then say "rolling" or something similar (not "action"—you are not making a movie). At this point, a little red light comes on above the lens. Ignore it and **speak to the person asking the questions. Do not look or glance into the camera.** This is easy in a studio, where you can hardly see any cameras because of all the bright lights. Be aware that you will need makeup for a studio interview, but remember that blushes don't show on TV.

When you are introduced, just smile and keep looking directly at the interviewer. Don't reply with, e.g., "Good morning, Valerie; it's a pleasure to be here," as this will make you sound like a politician. Don't be tempted to look at all the movement going on around you in the studio.

Managing

191

Treat radio, television and newspaper interviews the same way. If the event in which you are involved or on which you are commenting is deemed "newsworthy" (i.e., is not just for "background"), everything you say matters. In this case, there is no such thing as "off the record," although you can insist on being quoted "without attribution" (i.e., anonymously).

The Golden Rules of interviewing are:

> Get your predetermined message across
> Don't let the interviewer put words in your mouth
> Don't refer to other people's business
> Don't mention politics
> Avoid sounding defensive
> Don't interrupt

... **speaking in public**

Coordinating humanitarian aid efforts in Yogyakarta, Indonesia, involved speaking to over 150 people packed into a rented hotel conference room night after night. Such conditions are not unusual in disaster situations. What you say and how you say it matters—those attending expect you to be knowledgeable and decisive. The secret lies in thorough preparation and delegating to others. Knowing how to use a microphone helps too.

When you are speaking in front of an audience, you are performing as an actor is onstage. Look pleasant, enthusiastic, confident, proud, but not arrogant. Avoid personal pronouns by saying "we," not "I."

Appear relaxed, even though you will feel nervous. Secretly, **take ten really deep breaths before starting**.

Memorize your first few sentences having first written down a key memory-jogging word for each.

Speak slowly, enunciate clearly. Speak to the person farthest away from you to ensure your voice is loud enough to project to the back of the room. Vary the tone of your voice.

If you are using a microphone, hold it away from and slightly below your mouth. Remember to switch it off when you have finished. When speaking, try to use a clip-on mike so that both hands can be free to gesticulate and arrange your papers.

Standing or moving about is preferable to sitting down.

Know how to use PowerPoint, especially how to start and stop the presentation, how to maximize, how to scroll (arrow keys) and how to blank the main screen while still being able to see the slide on the computer screen (hit the letter B or the F5 button).

Do not dazzle your audience with excessive use of animation, sound clips or gaudy colors that are inappropriate for your topic. Do not torture your audience by putting a lengthy document in tiny print on an overhead and reading it out to them.

Speak in a logical progression from introduction through strong supporting arguments to conclusion.

If you make an error, correct it and continue. There's no need to make excuses or apologize profusely.

Use eye contact to make everyone in your audience feel involved. George Clooney says it helps to focus on the forehead rather than the eyes when making an Oscar-acceptance speech!

Avoid humor in multicultural settings; not everyone will understand your joke and some may be offended by it.

Be sure all necessary equipment is set up and in good working order prior to the presentation.

Check out the location ahead of time to be sure of the seating arrangements.

Have handouts ready and give them out at the appropriate time—not at the beginning or your audience will be reading them rather than listening to you. Tell the audience ahead of time that you will be passing out an outline of your presentation so that they will not waste time taking unnecessary notes during your presentation.

To end your presentation, summarize your main points. Terminate your presentation with the single "bumper sticker" idea that you want your audience to remember. Then thank your audience and sit down.

... VIP visits

The European Commissioner for Humanitarian Affairs made her first official visit to Sarajevo at the height of the siege in the winter of 1995. As the only EC "official" in Bosnia-Hercegovina at the time, it fell to me to arrange her trip. In a country where electricity was intermittent, fuel and vehicles difficult to obtain, and such hotel rooms as there were had no running water or glass in the windows, this presented me with something of a logistics nightmare. Despite the presence of an unannounced entourage of jobsworthy commission "functionnaires," the three-day mission nevertheless passed off relatively incident free, with government meetings, press conferences, and project visits to schools and hospitals all going more or less as planned.

The EC was then "dumping" its Common Agricultural Policy surpluses on the unsuspecting Bosnians in the form of cans of gray, watery and dubious-looking beef. I remember drawing up in a convoy of six large white 4x4 cars, complete with police sirens and flashing blue lights, to visit a little old lady who lived alone with her cats in one of the more exposed suburbs.

The commissioner had expressed a wish to meet "real people and deserving beneficiaries of EC aid"—"discreetly, James, discreetly." So much for that. Numerous international TV network crews filmed the *Gospodjica* as she bent down outside her front door and, completely unfazed by the fuss and bustle around her, told the assembled dignitaries to wait while she finished feeding her cats . . . on the EC canned beef.

We then went indoors to spend the next thirty minutes drinking ersatz tea while the old lady forcefully explained to the head of European Humanitarian Affairs that most of the food she was responsible for supplying was fit only for animals!

Being told you are responsible for organizing a VIP visit should fill you with dread. It is one of those little things in life that no one thanks you for if it goes flawlessly but everyone delights in blaming you for if it all goes awry. High-level diplomatic visits will have embassy staff running around ignoring you. It nevertheless falls to you to make sure everything goes as planned. When multiple agencies are involved, each will take responsibility for their own delegation; it merely falls to you to provide overall coordination. Here is a basic checklist of key tips that help such visits go less rockily than they otherwise might:

> Ascertain exactly who is coming and with what size and type of entourage, the arrival and departure dates, who and what they want to see, and what outcome is expected of the visit. Your advice will probably be requested about people to see and projects to visit. It is quite normal for all these details to change radically a few hours before the delegation is due to arrive, so have a Plan B.

> Formally inform the host government's "protocol office" (normally located somewhere inside the prime minister's Secretariat).

> Inform the chief of police, so that he can begin to make security arrangements. He will appreciate the heads-up and become your friend—always useful. Assume the VIP will be traveling with armed close protection and check whether weapons clearances or other permits are needed.

> Ask the chief of police (and/or the UN) to provide two dedicated radio frequencies for your exclusive use for "command and control" during the visit. These are crucial and must be in addition to any being used by embassies, the military or government departments. When the VIPs arrive, it is up to you, as the principal coordinator, to call "wheels down." This establishes you as the boss—command and control is now exercised by you alone. Despite the presence of cell phones, most decisions will be passed by radio, as texting takes too long.

> Inform the head of the airport. He can begin to arrange airside passes and press conference facilities. Try not to allow these to take place on the airport tarmac.

> Beg 4x4 cars from partner agencies, as you will never have enough. When planning seat allocation, allow only two VIPs per car (plus two "advisers"). Have two cars as "spares"; one will always break down and the other will be needed for the hapless person who somehow finds that his vehicle has driven off without him. There is always one. On initial pickup at the airport, arrange for one covered and lockable truck for luggage and one 20-seat minibus for assorted hangers-on and media, who nobody told you were coming.

> Each vehicle must have a number taped to the inside of the windshield. This is also the vehicle's call sign. Each driver must have signed for a handheld VHF radio plus spare battery. The visit program must always include details of who is to get into which number car.

> Book five more hotel rooms than you need. Arrange a secondary backup location, too, just in case.

> Plans tend to change at the end of the day—around midnight. Make sure you can print the program changes that follow in the hotel business center or manager's office, as these will need to be slipped under each visitor's door in the early hours of the morning. These visits are a never-ending flurry of program changes. The only way to let everyone know is to be constantly printing and distributing new programs. Make sure the version, date and time of production is clear in the footer. Alert everyone that there have been changes by text.

> Have a conference first thing every morning with everyone involved in making logistical arrangements. Have one person responsible for separately briefing the drivers. Once "wheels up" is declared (when the VIPs have left the country), be sure to debrief everyone involved before retiring for a well-earned drink. Not only will this give you the chance to thank people you will need on your side again one day but it also ensures that loaned equipment finds its way back to the owners.

REALITY CHECK

One VIP visit I arranged was by a delegation of European parliamentarians to Rwanda. Their mission was to observe the appalling water-supply situation in Kigali for themselves so that they could go back to Brussels informed with firsthand knowledge of the problem. Having ensured that they arrived at their hotel dusty and sweaty after an afternoon in the field, I waited in the lobby for the deluge of complaints that I knew was coming my way: "James, there is no water… the showers do not work." I politely told each dignitary in turn that water supply in Kigali was indeed sometimes erratic and that perhaps they might consider taking a swim instead. What they didn't know was that, for the greater good of Rwanda, I had persuaded the hotel manager not only to turn off the water supply but also to close the pool so that these cosseted visitors got a taste, just a small taste, of what living without water was really like. Weeks later, the aid budget for Kigali's water treatment and distribution system passed without amendment through the Humanitarian Aid Committee of the European Commission.

... **hiring and firing**

Hiring national or international staff locally can be something of a lottery. Half the time, you will hire someone who excels in the job and makes you look good. But the other half, you will hire someone who lets you down two months later and makes you look bad. You can improve the odds by being ruthless when short-listing candidates for interview on the strength of their CVs. Look at neither age nor gender but only the degree to which their qualifications and experience match the specifications of the job. Make a judgment about their emotional suitability (EQ) as well, not just their intelligence (IQ). Prior to interviewing, ask the candidates to send an example of their recent work. Read this, and be prepared to quiz the candidate, not on the contents as such but on why and how it was written.

The purpose of the interview is to ascertain why short-listed candidates really left their past positions, whether they really did what they say they did, to judge their flexibility and willingness to work beyond the basic job description, their attitudes to your authority and whether you think they will fit within your current management structure. Interviews are only useful if they get behind a participant's experiences. This is achieved by pursuing in-depth information around a topic by asking preformulated yet open-ended questions (the same open-ended questions are asked to all), with respondents free to choose how to answer the question. This approach facilitates faster interviews that can be more easily analyzed and compared. In terms of **process**:

> Choose a setting with little distraction.
> Explain who you are (the interview panel should always be more than one person, with at least one woman) and the purpose of the interview.
> State that the interview is confidential, and confirm that the interviewee is happy to have references followed up.
> Explain the format of the interview, and how their answers will be analyzed. If you want them to ask questions, specify when they're to do so.
> Indicate how long the interview usually takes.
> Ask them if they have any questions before you get started.

In terms of the questions to be asked, note the difference between fact and opinion in the responses, and pose them in terms of past, present or future. In terms of **sequence**:

> Get the respondent involved in the interview as soon as possible.

> Before asking about controversial matters (such as feelings and conclusions), first ask about some facts. With this approach, respondents can more easily engage in the interview before warming up to more personal matters.

> Five questions are sufficient. Each one should follow the basic pattern: "Give an example of x; what you did; why you did it; what you would have done differently; and how you applied the lessons learned." Of the five questions, two should be on "competences" (such as "integrity" or "leadership"), with the remainder based on technical knowledge.

> The final questions should be: "Is there anything you would like to add or highlight, and is there anything you would like to ask us?"

In terms of **hints for interviewers**:

> Attempt to remain as neutral as possible. That is, don't show strong emotional reactions to the candidates' responses.

> Encourage responses with occasional nods of the head, "uh-huhs," etc.

> Be careful about the appearance of your note-taking. That is, if you jump to take a note, it may suggest that you're surprised or very pleased about an answer, which may influence answers to future questions.

> Provide transition between major topics, e.g., "We've been talking about [some topic] and now I'd like to move on to [another topic]."

> Don't lose control of the interview. This can occur when respondents stray to another topic for too long.

> Write down any observations made during the interview. For example, was the respondent particularly nervous at any time? Were there any surprises during the interview?

> Grade each candidate with marks out of ten against specific criteria, such as "Was the question answered?"; "Was the response too wordy?"

For the person being interviewed, more and more human resources departments are hiring people who "give good interview" rather than those who have the most appropriate technical qualifications or experience. This trend is giving rise to a risk-averse culture within organizations, which appears to be accelerating. Mostly, this is the result of questions being posed that focus on "core competencies" such as "leadership" and "challenges faced" rather than demonstrable evidence of outcomes that positively affect real people.

A typical interview follows a predictable pattern:

1. **"Summarize your career to date"**: focus here on three successes involving teams.

2. **"What can you bring to our organization?"**: highlight three core strengths that you know from your preparatory researches are what the potential employer is looking for.

3. **"Give us an example of when you were involved in a difficult negotiation. What was the outcome? What would you now do differently?"**: you can expect four such questions, each covering a different topic but using the same format. You are being assessed as much for your ability to answer the question in a logical and timely manner without waffling as for the content of your response.

Unless you are closing down a program—in which case everyone is losing their job—firing an individual for poor performance is unpleasant for all concerned. Such an event should not take place without there first having been two formal notifications: the first oral, the second in writing. The latter should have involved written appraisal against expected and agreed deliverables.

This having been done, politely point out where the employee in question has failed to deliver and ask him or her for any comments in each case. Always make it clear that the employee is not being let go for incompetence, but because he or she has particular skills

Let the employee know (s)he is being let go not for incompetence but because his or her particular skills no longer fit the program or organization at this time.

that no longer fit the program or organization at this particular time. Make it clear whether or not you will be supplying a reference. As with hiring, always have another person with you when conducting these interviews. At least one person should be female. This prevents later allegations of abuse of position or even sexual harassment. When letting drivers or warehouse staff go, make sure that all vehicle, warehouse and office keys are accounted for first. Take extra precautions—it's not unknown for copies to have been secretly made.

... **local authorities**

REALITY CHECK

At the beginning of the last crisis in Lebanon, a UN coordinator called a meeting to order without first introducing his national counterpart from the Lebanese Ministry of Health. Worse, he failed to acknowledge the presence of the Hezbollah representative, who, despite not being "official," had been working in partnership with the government for years. Both stood up and challenged the coordinator's authority to convene such a meeting, and went on to challenge the authority of the entire UN system, which soured relations across all sectors for some time.

International staff often forget that they are in a disaster- or conflict-affected country as guests. Even permanent UN staff are guests of the host government, while the agencies they work for are officially invited to be present in the country by the government. Local authorities are therefore in charge, at least in principle.

Given that they have often been rendered as dysfunctional as the citizens they represent by the crisis, they are usually only too happy for experienced agency representatives to offer advice on response and mitigation measures. This often extends to running day-to-day coordination of external aid inputs, at least in the short term. In such cases, **the aim should always be to share and then hand back these responsibilities at the first possible moment**. The story above, although unusual, should always be borne in mind, as it demonstrates the danger of assuming too much and not knowing enough about local geopolitical realities.

... the military

Most civilians tend to view anyone in uniform as a brainwashed killing machine incapable of original thought. They are also thought of as all the same, whichever "arm" they belong to and whatever their experience. For their part, military people tend to see aid workers as adrenaline-addicted social misfits incapable of getting a regular job at home. At least, these are the stereotypes. Like all stereotypes, both are wrong. As with any profession, language creates a barrier to those who don't know the code. Both the military and the aid community excel at inventing an alphabet soup of acronyms that make mutual understanding more complicated than it need be.

Civilians, whether they be humanitarian workers, journalists or members of the business and development world, must realize that soldiers are not all the same: armored regiments work and think differently from infantry battalions, for example—they are different sizes too. An American marine is not the same as a British marine, and a naval captain is a higher rank than an army captain. Military personnel, for their part, should understand that while some aid workers are indeed unpaid volunteers, the majority are highly qualified in what they do and have many years of experience working with affected populations in developing countries.

This section should help debunk some of the myths.

In cases where a properly mandated international military force is present on the ground, it will usually be necessary for humanitarian organizations to have a means of dialogue with that force. At the simplest level, this may be only for information on the security situation, for example. It also provides the opportunity to remind one another of respective roles and activities, including obligations under international humanitarian law.

Humanitarian organizations should take care that their contact with any military force is not perceived as compromising their independence and impartiality. In most cases, this will probably mean that contact with any military body should be low profile.

Some humanitarian organizations believe that military forces should never provide any humanitarian assistance or support to humanitarian organizations, on the grounds that this compromises humanitarian independence and confuses the military and humanitarian roles in the minds of the local population. Others believe that, in cases where humanitarian organizations are overwhelmed by serious need, it may be right for the military to support the humanitarian effort in order to save life and prevent suffering. The majority view is that military forces should help with a humanitarian effort only in urgent, life-or-death situations where humanitarian organizations are not able to meet the need.

If the military does provide support to the humanitarian effort, it should clearly be in support of humanitarian organizations and provided at their request. Such assistance has in the past included:

> Rapid construction of refugee camps and associated facilities (though usually to military norms, which are inappropriate for large civilian populations and are usually below internationally accepted construction standards as a result)
> Convoy protection (into "safe zones" and along "humanitarian corridors," as in central Bosnia)
> Area security (as in Afghanistan)
> Responding to emergency security needs
> Logistics assistance (e.g., road repair, bridge building, helicopter support, bulk distribution of relief commodities)
> Mine clearance
> Medical assistance
> Threat assessment

In the past decade, western and northern military alliances such as NATO have taken on a "peace support" operational role in addition to fighting wars. This has given new responsibilities to senior commanders, including negotiating with factional leaders and local government officials, managing civil–military relations and securing a safe environment for humanitarian programs.

This has demanded the ability to engage with people outside the military, including with representatives of nongovernmental and international organizations, and assumes knowledge of geopolitics, cultural awareness, foreign languages and civilian interpersonal skills. In other words, exactly the same skill sets as any senior manager within an aid organization.

Military officers understand and respect this. They also respect the fact that aid workers are required to work in difficult and dangerous situations with no protection except their neutrality. In return, the military expect aid workers to respect the complexities of their modern war-fighting and peace-building roles and to recognize that attainment of "rank" is not automatic (as most civilians mistakenly think) but dependent on ability.

The simplest way to do this is to **know the difference between a captain, a major, a colonel and a general, and to call them by their rank. If in doubt, just call anyone older than you "sir"**; it does not make you subservient, it is just what they are used to. You should call anyone below the rank of colonel by their first name. The normal rank structure more or less follows the pattern below (UN-equivalent grades are in parentheses):

One or two "stars" or "pips" = lieutenant (P2)

Three stars = captain (P3)

Crown = major (P4)

Crown and one star = lieutenant colonel (P5)

Crown and two stars = colonel (P5)

Crown and three stars = brigadier (D1)

Anything with either crossed swords or large amounts of gold "spaghetti" = general (D2)

Captain

Major

Lieutenant Colonel

Colonel

Brigadier General

NATO

U.S.

Regiments or battalions are commanded by lieutenant colonels and are made up of usually four squadrons (for cavalry) or companies (for infantry), each commanded by a major. Each squadron is made up of three or four troops (cavalry) or platoons (infantry). These are commanded by lieutenants or, depending on their size or function, captains.

Battlegroups are composite forces based around a regimental or battalion headquarters, and comprise a variety of infantry companies, armored squadrons, engineer units and an artillery battery, depending on their role.

It helps to know your military hardware and some limited military terminology. Soldiers expect you to know basic vehicle types. That tanks have large barrels and are used primarily to destroy other tanks. Self-propelled artillery pieces look similar but have larger turrets and larger fume extractors halfway down the barrel. Everything else with armor is an "armored fighting vehicle" (AFV) or "armored personnel carrier" (APC). These are usually infantry-carrying and have a smaller turret and smaller gun.

Troop carrier

Tank

Artillery

"Indirect fire" is that fired with no line of sight to the target, from mortars or artillery

"Direct fire" is when the shooter can see the target

RPG = Rocket Propelled Grenade

LZ (pronounced "ell zee") = Landing Zone for parachute insertion

HLS = Helicopter Landing Site

RV = Rendezvous Point

(T)AOR = (Tactical) Area of Responsibility

ETA/D = Estimated Time of Arrival/Departure

NEWD = Night Exercise Without Darkness

TEWT = Tactical Exercise Without Troops

CP = Command Post

OP = Observation Post

FAC = Forward Air Controller (who directs ground-attack aircraft to their targets)

"Bracketing" = when a mortar or artillery round lands in front of you and then another behind. Halving the difference in elevation at the firing end means the third round is almost bound to hit you. It can take as little as twenty seconds to adjust the aim and allow for time of flight of the projectile.

You will often hear military people, when talking among themselves, referring to "J-something." It refers to general staff officer functions as follows:

J1 = personnel and manning

J2 = intelligence

J3 = operations and training

J4 = logistics

J5 = planning

J6 = communications

J7 = military assistance (press and civil affairs)

Being "operational" in nature, the J2 and J3 functions are taken more seriously by nonmilitary people than the others. Almost all tactical commanders in the field will have passed through these disciplines at some point in their careers.

Reference to "SO1," "2" or "3" just means that the subject is a staff officer engaged in planning rather than operations. The numbers equate to ranks, with 1 being the highest. In combined "stabilization" or "integrated" missions where military, political, development and humanitarian groups work alongside one another, these positions influence the way operations are carried out, so mutual understanding of respective roles and responsibilities should be carefully cultivated.

When communicating with military personnel, it is useful to put as much data on a map as possible. This form of visual representation is easily understood by the military and is usually appreciated, as it is concise and avoids confusion over locations and who is doing what where. Relevant data from the military can also easily be added to it.

... negotiation and resolving conflict

REALITY CHECK

I was negotiating access to the rebel-held areas of North Darfur so that the polio-eradication campaign could continue. We had been at it all day, sitting under a bush in the desert, surrounded by well-armed and silent gunmen wearing dark glasses and *shamargs*, which covered their faces. The leader understood the importance of polio-eradication efforts but was suspicious of WHO's intentions, continually saying that the vaccine was a poison sent from their "enemy" in Khartoum. I would not compromise, saying that the vaccines were property of the United Nations and, as such, were representative of the independent and neutral values of the worldwide humanitarian system.

We solved the problem by agreeing, amid much tension, to each choose a sample from the cold-box at random and give it to each other. I agreed to go first, but only on condition that the leader also did so within ten minutes. The key that unlocked the negotiation was that I had a large bag of oranges on the kilim at my feet, which I offered to share but only when we reached agreement. Judging by their laughter when we eventually did, the rebels had not seen, let alone eaten, an orange for many months. I always take fruit with me now, and there have been no reported cases of polio since in that difficult part of Sudan.

We are all negotiating all the time. Sometimes it's "hard" negotiation, such as negotiating access to rebel-held areas. Sometimes it's "soft" negotiation, such as handling disagreements among the staff. The principles are the same though. Negotiation isn't about winning and it isn't about someone else losing. It is about learning to "play the game," and, as with any game, there are rules and conventions. Here are three:

> Know what the other side wants
> Know how much you can give away
> Read body language so that you know when to make demands and when to compensate

There are typically three behavioral strategies that people instinctively use when faced with disagreement. None of them help in any way to resolve conflict or deal with difficult people effectively. They are designed to make us feel better, or at least justified in our feelings and actions. But they don't change the situation and almost always make it worse. Don't:

> get aggressive
> talk to the wrong people
> assume the other person is wrong

In addition, negotiators often become victims to the personalities and communication styles of their interlocutor. It is better to take charge of the relationship and manage it, instead of letting it manage you. This means **changing what you do, what you say and how you say it**. This will change the dynamic between you and the other person. You may not always get what you want, but you will certainly be in charge of what happens between the two of you.

Here are some principles you could apply to help resolve conflict and get on better with your problem person:

> Figure out what's really going on
> Deal with things as they arise
> Blame your position on superiors far away
> Moderate your language and keep your voice low
> Set clear boundaries
> Make the point early on that you are prepared to walk away

Managing

207

When you are negotiating in foreign languages, interpreters will be needed. Choose yours carefully, as you need diplomatic skills as much as you need the languages. To be effective, interpreters must also be independent. This means giving consideration to gender, ethnicity, family ties and political affiliation when hiring. In particularly tricky negotiations, you may need to monitor what your interlocutor is having translated to make sure that the opposing interpreter is not injecting his or her biases into the negotiation. Choose an interpreter who has the potential to become a friend. Having spent many smoke-infused mornings talking to obstinate generals and having dodged a few Bosnian bullets with me, my Croat interpreter remains a close friend of mine some twenty years after we worked together.

... influencing people

Years ago, my ex-wife taught me a "missing coin" trick in which I appear to make a coin vanish into my arm. There are commercially available tricks that do similar things. Such tricks amaze children anywhere in the world, rich and poor alike, and are guaranteed to create a warm atmosphere. I have used my trick to impress a minister of state and numerous village heads. Be warned, though: If demonstrating "magic" in more out-of-the-way villages, always show the village head the trick beforehand. He will quickly forget how to do it, but it enhances his status in the village and prevents trouble later when everybody thinks you are some kind of witch doctor.

Mention has been made previously of "adaptors" for soccer balls. These are the little thin tubes of metal that can connect a bicycle pump to a deflated ball (and cost pennies each). Bicycle pumps and soccer balls can be found in even the most isolated communities throughout Africa and South America—though less so in South and Southeast Asia, where cricket is the more universal passion. But the local children are nearly always to be found playing with some newspaper wrapped up with string and condoms instead. This is because they have no means to inflate the soccer ball. Having such an adaptor in my pocket has opened doors that talk alone would have taken all day to open. To this day, for example, I am waved to the front of the line of vehicles on the border between Rwanda and Uganda because the border guards, always in need of a new adaptor, recognize me. As with the magic tricks, be aware that the donation of such "gifts" interferes with local power dynamics, so be careful with whom you share your largesse.

Being able to play a musical instrument guarantees you access to the best parties—especially in isolated places. If that is beyond you, at least **know the words and tune to a song**. Even if you can't sing, it is the effort that counts. Your national anthem will suffice, or if you're feeling adventurous, a bawdy song always goes down well—complete with hand gestures.

REALITY CHECK

I had had a particularly trying day to the south of Brčko in Central Bosnia during the Bosnian War in the midnineties. My desk officer, a young and innocent female bureaucrat from Brussels, was accompanying me on an assessment mission, and we had spent much of the afternoon cowering in concrete passageways trying to avoid the artillery rounds exploding around us. We eventually arrived in the darkened town of Tuzla after curfew, dirty, exhausted and badly needing something to eat. There was nothing in the hotel except potatoes, so we set off to look for a little basement café I knew nearby, more in hope than expectation of finding something more sustaining. As we splashed through the slushy darkness, all was ghostly quiet. Not a light was to be seen—a feature of Bosnian towns in those days; like everything else, electricity was in short supply, and to show a light was to invite more Serbian shelling. Stumbling down the café steps, I opened the door, pushed back the heavy drapes inside and ushered my "boss" into the warmth and light. Absolute silence.

There in front of us, crammed into the tiny room, were at least one hundred fully armed, uniformed and battle-hardened soldiers of the Bosnian Fifth Corps on their way to the front at Srebrenica (later to go down in infamy as the scene of the worst massacre in post–Second World War Europe). Guns of all sorts were propped against the walls, with more vying for space among the numerous bottles of *slivovica* (locally distilled plum brandy) and plates of bread and *prsut* (smoked ham) littering the trestle tables. This was no place for me, far less a nubile young woman. One hundred pairs of eyes swiveled hungrily toward her. "Come on" I whispered. "Let's go." But before we had the chance to turn and duck back out through the drapes behind us, a loud voice called out, "Gospodin, [Mr.] James!"

I had been recognized. I turned nervously to find the mayor, a middle-aged and heavyset man with bucolic cheeks, waving us over. Clearly the worse for drink, he insisted we stay and made way for us on the bench beside him, knocking over a couple of AK-47s as he did so. A respected man, he knew me from previous negotiations about funding for humanitarian relief, which I suspected was doing little more than sustain the very soldiers now surrounding us. I was the "adviser" from the European Commission, and here I was introducing the actual decision-making "donor" all the way from the money bags of Brussels. "There'll be no getting away from here now," I thought. And there wasn't.

The mayor rose unsteadily to his feet and shouted across the rising noise of one hundred men intent on getting back to the serious business of singing and drinking before marching off to war, "A toast!" Everyone toasts everyone else in the Balkans at any opportunity, and failure to down copious shots of *slivovica* each time one is proposed is a grave social offense. And the rather frightened lady clinging to my left arm was a teetotaler! Nothing much happened, so he clambered on to the table and shouted again.

"This lady has come all the way from Brussels to give us money!" He raised his glass high. "To the European Community who have come to save us!" One hundred voices roared, "To the European Community!" and one hundred throats guzzled yet more large quantities of almost neat alcohol. We were "okay" now, the mayor having endorsed us as "friends of Bosnia."

After I made some rather lame toast in reply—I could hardly raise a glass to "your glorious victory" after all, since humanitarianism is all about neutrality and impartiality—the singing started in earnest. I knew my turn would come eventually, and it did. Meanwhile, one by one, soldiers would sidle up to my colleague and chat her up. Usually this included some offer of money. Despite the fact that she was not drinking, the alcohol fumes and the cigarette smoke were making her "tipsy" and she was beginning to enjoy herself. And so it was, with a drunken mayor trying to buy my boss, blinded by cigarette smoke, my attempt to soak up the *slivovica* by eating large chunks of bread having come to naught, and wearing a recently captured Serb officer's astrakhan hat, that I found myself swaying on a tabletop singing to one hundred cheering soldiers. I sang a variation of the best-known of all rugby songs, "Sweet Chariot," and I did it with all the rude hand gestures. But I did it in English and, having listened relatively politely, they wanted it again in Serbo-Croat.

With the mayor standing beside me, translating line by line, the soldiers, now comprehending what I was singing, went crazy. I had to do it again, this time explaining the links between the words and the hand gestures. The soldiers went crazier still and began to sing along. I lost count of how many times we sang that night, but I do remember that it was difficult to talk in the morning.

All of which would have been fine were it not for the fact that, unknown to me, the local Tuzla radio station had been there to record the mayor's speech (which we missed) and had recorded the sing-along. On my return, weeks later, I was told that the song had not only become the battle anthem of the Bosnian Fifth Corps but was also regularly broadcast on local radio networks all over Eastern Bosnia. I denied my connection at the time, of course. So much for neutrality. But I am convinced that we escaped serious harm that night on account of singing this song. And we got fed too.

... body repatriation

When someone dies abroad, particularly if the death was sudden or unexpected, it is often difficult to know how to deal with the practical matters you need to address. Every country has its own formalities to be followed. The purpose of the following information is to set out the general process and rules involved when repatriating a body for burial or cremation. I wish I had had this information to guide me through those awful two days in Split (see "reality check" on page 212).

Make sure the embassy or embassies of the deceased are informed. Diplomats will arrive as quickly as they can to take over the arrangements. Establish contact with the country directors of the aid organizations to which the deceased belonged.

Say nothing to the media except how tragic has been the waste of life in furtherance of the service of others, how proud you are to have worked with the deceased and how your thoughts and prayers go out to their family/families.

Repatriation of the remains of a deceased person is a complicated and costly process. **Embassies will not pay, so make sure you find out who will before signing anything.** There is a lot of paperwork. You may be involved in obtaining most of the following:

> consent for repatriation from next of kin (NOK)
> death certificate

> police letter
> burial permission
> embalming certificate
> clearance of payment
> list of belongings
> original passport
> medical certificate giving cause of death
> certification as to whether a postmortem examination has been carried out or not
> authorization to remove the body from any third country
> certificate to the effect that the body is not coming from an area of infectious disease

Before any arrangements can be made to repatriate a body, it will be necessary to have the remains formally identified. That is, the identity of the deceased must be officially confirmed in line with the laws in the country in which the death took place. The rules on who may formally identify a deceased person can vary, but usually identification may be carried out by a colleague of the deceased. Depending on local laws and rules, however, it may be necessary for a family member to travel to the place where the deceased is to confirm the identity.

REALITY CHECK

I was in Split, Croatia, when the call came through that a number of Danish colleagues had been killed while escorting a humanitarian aid convoy outside Zenica in Central Bosnia and that their bodies were arriving by helicopter that afternoon. "Would I please deal with the formalities." I had no idea of the moral or legal implications. I didn't know whether their families had been informed. I didn't know if there were protocols to follow. I didn't even know for sure who they were. All I did know was that I had been with these wonderful people only days before. There can be no more serious—and no more upsetting—a business than repatriating bodies of friends and colleagues. For, in aid work, these people were often "representing" the agency they work for, if not their country. They also died defenseless in pursuance of an ideal and they deserve the dignity and respect that this implies.

In order to obtain the release of the body for repatriation from the authorities in the country where the person died, you should **appoint a funeral director** in that country. A funeral director is someone whose business it is to prepare the dead for burial and to arrange and manage funerals. Services of funeral directors are not free, so you should check the costs associated prior to engaging these services. The local funeral director will prepare the body for repatriation, prepare the appropriate documentation and obtain the death certificate. S/he can also make all the necessary flight arrangements in cooperation with the embassy concerned.

If the death was not natural, it will be referred to a coroner, who will open an inquest to investigate the cause and circumstances of death.

Funeral arrangements should not be confirmed until the coroner's office has cleared the documentation. International regulations (Article 3 of the League of Nations International Regulations concerning the conveyance of corpses, 1937, and the Council of Europe Agreement on the Transfer of Corpses, 1973) require all coffins crossing international frontiers by air or sea to be metal (zinc or lead)-lined and sealed. The deceased must also be embalmed.

Many relatives and friends of those killed in a disaster ask searching and detailed questions about exactly how the person died. Be prepared to **answer these as honestly as you know how**. Often, this is unlikely to satisfy the need to know how an individual met his or her death. People may feel that all was not done that should have been in order to satisfy their need for information, or that they are being denied information that was available. Don't take it personally; often grief is manifested as aggression.

After a disaster, regardless of the state of the body, family members may wish to have the opportunity to see that person before the remains are returned home or to the place of burial or cremation. You may have to facilitate this.

Allow the humanitarian community to pay their respects in some way. Some form of ceremony—probably religious—should be thought about. Contact a priest/imam to do this, according to known religious preference. This can be done at the airport on departure, if necessary.

... **medical evacuation**

Or "medevac," as it is known, is easy by comparison and will be handled between the medical (hospital) authorities and the insurance company, once you have ascertained who they are and put them in touch with each other. A doctor who has examined the patient must sign a certificate stating that medevac is necessary. This certificate must be faxed to the insurance company. It is always appreciated if you **contact the injured person's immediate family, too, and let them know what is going on.** If stabilization is required prior to movement, a family member may well fly out to visit. Accompany the injured person to the aircraft and get one of the accompanying paramedics to sign for all personal effects; somehow, personal possessions have a habit of disappearing en route. Make sure you have your colleague's passport.

REALITY CHECK

The "reality check" in the **broken limbs** section refers to the time I broke my back. Often forgotten in this saga is that one of my wonderful Pakistani colleagues in the office, Maha, had the password to my private email account, which meant she could access stored copies of all my personal details. With the help of my brother back in the U.K., she was able to arrange all aspects of my stabilization and eventual medical evacuation.

... **securing data**

Apart from their high resale value, laptops often contain sensitive business and personal information. It is vital, then, that you take precautions for protecting your laptop and the information on it.

Don't put your laptop in your checked luggage. Checking your laptop is a big gamble; always keep it with you. Keep your laptop inconspicuous and carry it in a nondescript case.

Attach your laptop to a fixed object with a purpose-built security cable, keep it in a lockable suitcase when you are not in the room or ask to put it in the hotel safe when you are not using it.

Do not log on to unsecured wireless networks. If the wireless network you're logging on to doesn't require you to enter a password, don't use it. Unsecured networks are a two-way street. While anyone can access the network, anyone on the network may be able to access your laptop, and subsequently your information.

Avoid accessing financial or banking records while traveling, especially on public wireless networks. This will help to prevent your bank records and financial information from ending up in the wrong hands.

Deselect "remember me" when browsing the Internet. Clicking "remember me" on websites, or allowing the Internet browser to remember passwords or user names, negates the security those user name and passwords offer. If a thief gets hold of your laptop, they will easily be able to steal your online (and possibly offline) data.

Back up valuable data before traveling. Back up your data as frequently as possible, to minimize the risk of data loss in the event that your laptop is stolen. A detachable 320 GB hard drive is what most people use, as it also allows "remote" working, i.e., the use of someone else's laptop. Windows 7 and Vista operating systems both include encryption options. Use them to back up sensitive or valuable files and keep the hard drive separate from your laptop.

In extremis, it may be prudent to destroy the hard drive. Unscrew it from the back of your laptop and smash it with a hammer. If you're really paranoid, pour acid from the car battery on what remains.

When working in very dusty or sandy conditions, such as in Darfur or eastern Chad, **wrap the keyboard in a single layer of plastic wrap**, as dust and sand can ruin nondigital hard drives in a matter of weeks. Make sure when doing so that ventilation holes are uncovered or the computer will overheat.

Checklists

what to pack

Apart from obvious things, like footwear, luggage, clothing, tents and bedding, all the items **highlighted in bold** are considered essential for anyone staying in places for any length of time where security is poor, disease incidence high and utilities unreliable.

For all

Waterbottle (empty)

Backpack (4,880 cubic inches/80 liters)

Daypack (600 cubic inches/10 liters): can double as a briefcase and emergency "go kit"

Cable padlock (combination type): for securing your belongings to something solid

Sturdy (ankle-supported) walking shoes (and spare laces)

Crush-proof jacket and tie/dress

2 x cold- or warm-weather clothing appropriate to the prevailing climate

Flip-flops

Cotton **robe**

Emergency rain poncho with hood (in compressed bag)

Sleeping bag (compressible, specified to 32°F/0°C): when using in conjunction with a silk liner (see below), it is not necessary to have a higher thermal rating (unless you will be living above 9,000 feet/3,000 meters)

Sleeping-bag liner (silk): better than cotton and can be used for both hot and cold climates

Pillowcase (cotton)

Compressed **foam mattress** (roll-up type): a **"cot"** raised off the ground is better but is too bulky to transport

Rubber door wedge: to wedge the door shut for security when sleeping

Sunglasses (and retaining strap)

Head lamp (and spare batteries)

Money belt: not a "pouch," one that looks like a belt

Toilet articles: shaving foam can be substituted by soap or oil

Map of where you're going

Dental floss: useful for hanging mosquito nets and sewing on buttons as well as flossing

Universal rubber bath plug: for bathing or shaving when there is a basin but no plug (and there never is)

Antibacterial soap bar (in a sealable dish or plastic bag)

Baby wipes (resealable packet of 50): for where water is scarce and washing difficult

Roll of toilet paper in waterproof bag: half the roll, squashed flat, will suffice

Large box (50) of tampons (or sanitary towels) in waterproof bag (for women only, obviously)

Earplugs and eyeshades: "beg" a set out of the business-class section when getting off your flight

Multitool (with corkscrew and pliers): *not* a penknife or Swiss Army knife as these are too weak and the blades too short for serious field use

Sewing kit: include a curved "suture needle" if possible

Laundry powder (8 ounces/250 g): I always regret it when I leave this out

Sunscreen (factor 40 or above): for use at high altitude as well as in the tropics

Lipscreen (total block): as above

Ball of string (preferably made from natural fiber)

2 x plastic bin liners (the sturdy ones): for keeping things dry

Waterproof matches (in a waterproof container)

Universal electrical adaptor: the Swiss Travel Products one works in all countries of the world, unlike some others

Water-purification tablets/drops

Insect repellent (roll-on, minimum 50 percent DEET)

Rimmed hat: not a baseball cap

Alarm clock (if not available on your cell phone or watch)

Compass: a small plastic one will suffice unless you are going trekking . . . in which case take a GPS

Wristwatch: keep it inexpensive (yet reliable) as an expensive-looking watch will end up getting you robbed. Try to avoid plastic straps, however, as these can "melt" into the skin when mixed with DEET (see insect repellent, above)

Whistle (plastic): for when you feel utterly alone and you hope people are out looking for you

Single **mosquito net** and 2 x elastic bungee cords

Cell phone (tri-band) and charger for home and car: plus international roaming SIM card, enabled

Portable rape/attack alarm with smoke detector: for hanging on the guesthouse door

Skype headset

Additional stuff for aid workers

Safari vest: the multipocket "vest" worn by big-game hunters in the movies (not a jacket)

3 x disposable dust masks: for working with dead bodies or when clearing post-earthquake rubble

Roll of plastic wrap or Saran Wrap: useful for wrapping laptop keyboards and cell phones in humid or dusty conditions

4 x nightlight candles (high density)

Roll of electrical tape

Dog tags (or certificate of blood group)

Clipboard (with rain cover), paper, colored pens

Set of water-soluble whiteboard markers (4 colors)

Personal file with detachable plastic sleeves

Flash memory (minimum 2GB)

Survival bag: for those hypothermia situations

Single-person tent

1 x meal ready-to-eat (MRE)

Small bottle of Tabasco and vegetable and/or chicken stock cubes

Optional items

Digital camera

GPS

Pocket binoculars

Laptop (with power-surge protector)

Laser pointer

Thuraya satellite phone

External hard drive (360 GB version): and download lots of movies and music before you go

Pocket calculator

Collapsible umbrella

6 x soccer-valve adaptors
Extra power source (e.g., powermonkey®)
Shortwave radio: consider a wind-up version

Paperwork (assuming these have all been scanned and emailed to yourself prior to departure)

Credit card
Passport (both if you have 2)
3 x photocopies of passport and visa (and residence permit)
8 x passport photographs (email a JPEG of a photo with a white background)
Travel tickets
Vaccination card
Yellow fever certificate (if separate from the vaccination card)
Driving license
Insurance contract and emergency number
List of important telephone numbers
3 x copy of Certificate of Advanced Security in the Field (if with the UN)

personal medical kit

Medical kits can only be of use if they contain the correct supplies, if the drugs are not time-expired and if the sterile items are still sterile. Knowing how to use the kit helps, of course, so attend a first-aid training session if you can.

Medication

Painkiller: 16 x acetaminophen 500 mg. tablets
Anti-diarrheal: 20 x Imodium/charcoal tablets
Oral rehydration salts: 6 x sachets (fruit-flavored)
Antibiotic: 20 x erythromycine 500 mg.
Antibiotic: 20 x amoxycillin 500 mg.
Antibiotic: 20 x ciprofloxacin 500 mg.
Antimalarial: 20 x Malarone 500 mg.
Antihistamine auto-inject (with vacuum sting remover)

Sterile equipment

1 x Infusion set
2 x catheters 18G 1¼"
2 x syringes 0.2 ml
2 x syringes 0.5 ml
2 x 25 needles 23G (0.6 mm)
2 x 25 needles 22G (0.7 mm)
10 x antiseptic cleaning wipes
Length of wide, self-adhesive cloth bandage
Spray-on "plastic" skin
First field dressing
2 x large bandages
Suture set

Pharmacy

12 x nonlubricated condoms
Roll-on insect repellent (with 50 percent minimum DEET)
Puritabs (or similar) for water treatment
Antiseptic: iodine/sulfonamide powder
Dermatological cream/foot powder
Eye ointment
Tweezers
Surgical scissors
6 x safety pins
Snake-bite vacuum pump
2 x surgical gloves
Butterfly stitches
IRM dental cement kit
Oil of cloves
Blood-clotting agent

"go kit"

This is an "emergency grab bag" (in a small daypack) that you should prepare and leave in a safe place (usually the bathroom) once you realize that rapid evacuation might become a reality.

Drinking water (4 liters)

Survival can (see next list)

Water-purification tablets (Puritabs)

3 x high-energy food bars

VHF handheld radio (and fully charged spare battery and car charger)

Thuraya satellite phone (incorporates GPS)

Compass

Regional map: you don't know far you will be going

Poncho

Space blanket

Photocopies of passport: take the original with you if you possibly can

survival can

It is best to make one up yourself, but they can be bought ready-made. If you are making up your own, use a sealable can and make sure your name is clearly marked on the top.

Fabric plasters (various sizes): don't use the plastic ones as they tend not to stick so well in sweaty conditions

Butterfly stitches: for not-quite-so-deep wounds

2 x sterile wipes: good as firelighters

Water-purification tablets (Puritabs)

Notepaper and pencil: with the pencil sharpened at both ends

Money (5 x US$10) sealed in a plastic bag

Wire saw: with a ring on each end through which a stick can be placed to make handles

Razor blade

Nightlight candle

Suturing needle: for sewing up people as well as sewing on buttons

Dental floss: better than string

4 x safety pins (medium)

Small (key-ring type) flashlight: with paper insulating the battery from its contact

Small multitool (e.g., Leatherman Juice)

Small compass

Fire-steel and flint

All-weather matches (in a sealed plastic bag)

5 x tampons soaked overnight in petroleum jelly (in a sealed plastic bag): great firelighters

Rabbit snare-wire

3 x nonlubricated condoms: for use as water containers or for keeping surprisingly large things dry

Fishing hooks (sizes 2, 3 and 6) and cast (10-lb breaking strain)

Roll of electrical tape

Space blanket (if there is any room left)

vehicle specification (4x4)

This is the optimum specification when traveling off-road for more than one day.

Full-length metal roof rack (plus ladder)

Cross-country tires fitted (snow or sand tires; 12-ply or more)

Winch (cable of 6-ton breaking strain): mounted on the front chassis, *not* the bull bar

Front and rear towing hooks

Reinforced suspension

Long-range fuel tank

Power-assisted steering

Air-conditioning unit and heater

Snorkel air intake

2 x sand-ladders (for desert use)

2 x extra headlights: plus wire mesh guards for all lights

Laminated windshield

Hi-Lift Jack (in addition to the hydraulic jack fitted as standard) and a board with a bolt through it

Wheel brace

Lockable wheel nuts (one per wheel)

Tow-rope

Snatch rope

Trauma kit: this should be suitcase-size; sealed, as it contains prescribed drugs; opened only in the event of an emergency; renewed every two years

2 x spare wheels (inflated and locked on roof)

4 x metal jerry cans of fuel (chained and locked to the roof rack)

4 x metal jerry cans of water (ditto)

Metal trunk (welded to the rear of the roof rack): lockable and water/dustproof

4 x snow chains (i.e., one per wheel)

Antiblast blanket: no good if it gets wet; you can use half-filled sandbags instead to line foot-wells

HF (Codan) and VHF radio fitted

GPS fitted

Windshield aerial for the Thuraya

2 x halon fire-extinguishers

Set of spare parts (bulbs, fuses, injectors/spark plugs, fuel filter and belts)

Tool kit (adjustable wrench, socket set, screwdriver set, pliers, hacksaw and spare blades, file, hose clips, electrical wire and connectors, roll of insulating tape)

Large can of tire-weld: this will temporarily fix a puncture

Foot pump: energy-consuming as it might be to reinflate a tire manually, don't bother with the small electrical pumps, which tend to burn out

Shovel: with one edge sharpened to act as a machete

Fueling hose with hand-pump

Plastic sheet and rope

Remote lamp (can be plugged into the cigar-lighter)

Map

Compass

Battery jump leads: not the high-street type but the high-tension cables used by truck drivers

Identifying markings and flag: plus a tube of the correct diameter welded to the roof rack in which to place the flagpole

2 x blankets

10-man meals ready to eat (MRE)

Vehicle documents, including: ownership documents; authorization documents; insurance certificate; vehicle logbook (for recording journeys made; to include columns for date, start location, time of departure, kilometer reading at departure, destination, time of arrival, kilometer reading at destination, purpose of trip, name of driver, signature); vehicle manual

"office in a box"

For establishing a temporary office in a tent or hotel room.

1 x corporate identity manual (CD-ROM) and templates (business cards, letters, file spines, etc.)

2 x flip charts (plus 4 x paper pads)

4 x four-color flip-chart pens

4 x whiteboards (5 x 4 feet) and color whiteboard pens

2 x cork boards (5 x 4 feet)

200 x blank business cards with agency name (and logo)

1 x multimedia projector (plus remote)

1 x projection screen (wall mountable)

1 x laptop and charger: pre-installed with Microsoft Office, Photoworks and Publisher

4 x 4MB flash drives

1 x color laser-jet printer (plus 6 x spare black ink cartridges, 3 x sets of spare color ink cartridges)

1 x portable scanner/printer/photocopier (plus 3 x spare ink cartridges)

1 x amplification package (amplifier, speaker, 3 x desk and 3 x radio microphones, plus spare batteries)

6 x reams of 8½ x 11 paper

4 x packets of map pins

1 x Dymo label machine (plus 2 x spare rolls)

1 x 1-m ruler

2 x In-tray sets

1 x cash box

1 x accounts book

2 x books of receipt vouchers

30 x various sizes of organization logo stickers

4 x flags (2 for vehicles)

2 x foldable filing cabinets

1 x lockable filing cabinet

1 x kettle

1 x large can instant coffee/tea/sugar

1 x laser pointer

2 x wall clocks

10 x binders

10 x file dividers
1 x desktop calculator
6 x large rolls of masking tape
4 x large rolls of packing tape (plus 1 x dispenser)
20 x blank-formatted CDs (plus labels)
40 x CDs of reference book(s) relevant to your sector of operations

Tent supplement (NB these items are in addition to the above)

1 x tent (6 x 4m)
3 x alpine tents (3-man)
1 x Portaloo (plus disinfectant and paper sufficient for 12 man-weeks)
2 x spade
1 x pickaxe
1 x portable shower
1 x generator (4 kVa) and spares pack
1 x toolkit
1 x portable air-conditioning unit

Information management

1 x laptop (widescreen): pre-installed with Microsoft Office Suite, ArcGIS
1 x color laser printer capable of 11 x 17 printing (plus 6 x spare black ink cartridges, 3 x sets of spare color ink cartridges)
3 x reams of 11 x 17 paper

Communication

- 6 x VHF handheld radios (plus chargers, spare batteries and programming software)
- 1 x conference-call telephone (plus 2 x remote mute switches)
- 4 x Quadri-band mobile phones (with international SIM cards and international dialing enabled, plus unlimited credit)
- 1 x R-BGAN (or equivalent)
- 2 x extension cables and multisockets (fused)
- 2 x power-surge capacitators (CPUs)
- 2 x Thuraya satellite phones (with international SIM cards and international dialing enabled, plus unlimited credit)
- 1 x wireless LAN router

local phrases to be translated on arrival

On arrival in a foreign country where you know none of the languages spoken, ask the first friendly person you meet to translate the following. This exercise normally inspires much hilarity all around and ensures a friend for life. It's also enough to get you by.

....

My name is . . . =

....

What is your name? =

....

Thank you =

....

Please =

....

I want to go to . . . =

....

Yes =

....

No =

....

Left =

Right =

Straight on =

Stop =

How much? =

Where is ... ? =

Take me to ... =

Which way to ... =

Can you teach me your language (over dinner)? =

Are you married? =

My partner will be here shortly =

Please bring me some toilet paper =

I need some food/water =

Let's go =

Now =

Wait a minute =

233

conversion tables

To convert	into	multiply by	
		(imperial–metric)	(metric–imperial)
inches	centimeters	2.54	0.39
feet	meters	0.31	3.28
miles	kilometers	1.61	0.62
sq. yards	sq. meters	0.84	1.19
pints	liters	0.47	2.13
pounds	kilograms	0.45	2.21
tons	tons	1.02	0.98
hectares	acres	2.47	0.4

1 nautical mile = 1.152 statute miles = 1.852 kilometers

1 kilogram = the weight of 1 liter

°Centigrade x 1.8 + 32 = °Fahrenheit

°Fahrenheit − 32 x 0.555 = °Centigrade

acronyms

ACP = Africa, Caribbean and Pacific
ACT = Artesunate-based Combination Therapies
AOR = Area Of Responsibility
ARI = Acute Respiratory Infection
ARV = Anti-Retrovirus (Anti-retroviral therapy)
CAP = Consolidated Appeals Process
CBO = Community-Based Organization
CHAP = Common Humanitarian Action Plan
CIDA = Canadian International Development Agency
CSB = Corn-Soya Blend
DALY = Disability Adjusted Life Year
DART = Disaster Assistance Response Team
DDR = Disarmament, Demobilization and Reintegration
DEET = Di-Ethyl Ethanol Toluamide
DFID = UK Department For International Development
DRR = Disaster Risk Reduction
ECHO = European Commission Directorate-General for Humanitarian Aid
ELISA = Enzyme-Linked Immuno-Absorbent Assay
EMOP = Emergency Operations (WFP)
EPI = Expanded Programme of Immunization
ETA/D = Expected Time of Arrival/Departure
FAO = Food and Agriculture Organization
FFW = Food-For-Work
FOB = Free On Board (at point of embarkation)
GAM = Global Acute Malnutrition (see also SAM)
GHDI = Good Humanitarian Donorship Initiative
HIPC = Heavily Indebted Poor Countries
HIV/AIDS = Human Immunodeficiency Virus/Acquired Immune Deficiency
    Syndrome
HPN = Humanitarian Practice Network (Overseas Development Institute)
ICRC = International Committee of the Red Cross
IDP = Internally Displaced Person
IED = Improvised Explosive Device
IFF = International Finance Facility
IFRC = International Federation of Red Cross and Red Crescent Societies
IHL = International Humanitarian Law
IMCI = Integrated Management of Childhood Illnesses

IMR = Infant Mortality Rate
I/N NGO = International/National Non-Governmental Organization
IO = International Organization
IOM = International Office for Migration
ITN = Insecticide-Treated Bed Nets
ITSH = Internal Transport, Storage and Handling
JICA = Japan International Cooperation Agency
LRRD = Linking Relief, Rehabilitation and Development
MCH = Mother and Child Health
MDG= Millennium Development Goal
MMR = Maternal Mortality Ratio
MOU = Memorandum Of Understanding
MRE = Meal Ready-to-Eat
MUAC = Mid Upper-Arm Circumference
NFI = Non-Food Item
OCHA = UN Office for the Coordination of Humanitarian Affairs
OFDA = Office for Foreign Disaster Assistance
ORS = Oral Rehydration Salts
OSOCC (virtual) = On-Site Operations Coordination Center (virtual)
PEM = Protein Energy Malnutrition
PEP = Post-Exposure Prophylaxis
PRA = Participatory Rural Appraisal
PRRO = Protection, Relief and Recovery Operation (WFP)
RRA = Rapid Rural Appraisal
SAM = Severe Acute Malnutrition (see also GAM)
SAR = Search And Rescue
SGBV = Sexual and Gender-Based Violence
SRSG = Special Representative to the (UN) Secretary-General
TA = Technical Assistant
TFC = Therapeutic Feeding Center
UN = United Nations
UNDP = United Nations Development Programme
UNHCR = United Nations High Commissioner for Refugees
UNICEF = United Nations Children's Fund
USAID = United States Agency for International Development
UXO = Unexploded Ordnance
VAM = Vulnerability Assessment and Mapping
VOICE = Voluntary Organizations in Co-operation in Emergencies
WFP = World Food Programme
WHO = World Health Organization

stress-buster kit

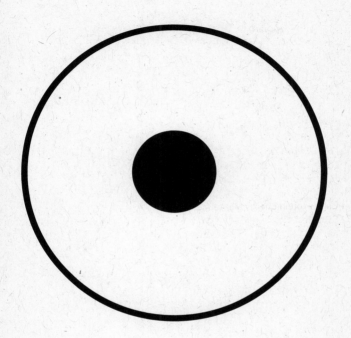

SIT DOWN AT YOUR TABLE OR DESK

KEEP THIS PAGE OPEN ON THE TABLE

LOOK CLOSELY AT THE BLACK DOT FROM ABOVE

SLOWLY BANG YOUR FOREHEAD ON CENTER DOT

REPEAT AS OFTEN AS NECESSARY

WHEN ASKED WHAT YOU'RE DOING, DENY EVERYTHING

James Shepherd-Barron has been an international aid worker and military peacekeeper for much of the past twenty-five years. Trained as a helicopter pilot for the British military, he has since served as a humanitarian affairs adviser for the United Nations, the U.K. government and the European Commission. He has lived and worked in more than twenty countries, including the conflict zones of Bosnia, Burundi, Iraq, Sudan, Lebanon and Pakistan.

James now runs a successful humanitarian affairs consultancy, working with clients such as DFID, the Red Cross, the World Health Organization and UNICEF. When not "on mission," he advises and trains senior UN, NGO and government operational staff in emergency health and coordination management.